AN EYE TO CHINA presents the reader with a confront-
ation between the perceptive imagination of a writer, and the
political phenomena of a new culture; a writer from a late
capitalist society, in decay in the mid-1970's, responding
with brilliance and subtlety to the vast social and political
transformations in the lives of one quarter of the world's
population.
Brought to the task, is a rare combination of literary skill
and political knowledge, to produce an undoubted masterpiece of materialist creation, in what could well prove to be,
also, a unique reconciliation of the main demands of politics
and art.

*"Here, the full apparatus of response has been fully exposed
to the shattering experience of the Chinese resumption of
history . . . few accounts can match this text in its penetration
of what the construction of a new culture consists of"*

Stuart Hall

*"In this powerful book, David Selbourne has gone beyond
reporting the new China, and has evoked its political and
human essence. The result is truer and fuller than volumes
of straight reporting"*

Neville Maxwell

BY THE SAME AUTHOR

PLAYS:

THE PLAY OF WILLIAM COOPER AND EDMUND DEW-NEVETT,
Methuen
THE TWO-BACKED BEAST, Methuen
DORABELLA, Methuen
SAMSON, Calder and Boyars
ALISON MARY FAGAN, Calder and Boyars
CLASS PLAY, Hutchinson
THE DAMNED, Methuen

ESSAYS:

BROOK'S DREAM, An Essay on the Politics of the Theatre, Action
Books
STATEMENT TO THE ROUNDHOUSE FORUM ON THE
POLITICS OF CULTURE, The Black Liberator, Vol. 1. No. 4
CLASS ENEMIES, DOUBTFUL CHARACTERS, and CLASS PLAYS,
Action Books, Texts for Study and Discussion

AN EYE TO CHINA

DAVID SELBOURNE

Introduction

STUART HALL

Photographs

CHARLES PARKER

TBL
PRESS

First published 1975
Copyright © David Selbourne, 1975
All rights reserved
Write to A.X. Cambridge, The Black Liberator Press,
67 Helix Road, London SW2, for all permissions
to reproduce

ISBN 0 905050 00 2

This book was collectively designed and produced by
A.X. Cambridge, Tony Hall, Gillian Noel, Lavern Richardson
and Lance Watson. It is set in Journal 10pt. type, and was
printed by The Selwyn-Maguire Printing Co., Ltd.,
3 Kelson Road, Westbury-on-Trym, Bristol

THE BLACK LIBERATOR PRESS is
a publishing offshoot of THE BLACK
LIBERATOR. Its purpose is to publish
texts which, in the judgement of the
Editorial Board, make a distinctive
contribution to an understanding of
contemporary World revolutionary
changes; or which provide new
evidence and analysis of the nature
and impact of imperialism and
racism, and of the international
and domestic class struggles being
waged against them.

In the event of any difficulties in
obtaining copies of this book, and
for ordering multiple copies at
special discount rates, write to
THE BLACK LIBERATOR PRESS

ACKNOWLEDGEMENTS

To Hazel Savage, source of ideas, who encouraged me to go to China; to Tong Hua-Ling, Han Yong-Liang, Li Cheng-Shsiao, and Lo Teh-Chuan, for information, interpretation, and re-interpretation; to Charles Parker, for his companionship in China; and to audiences at Ruskin College, Oxford, the Afro-Asian Society of the University of Sussex, Bicester School, and the Sheffield Library Theatre, for their responses to readings of parts of the draft text, which helped to guide the writing of the final versions.
Sections of the early drafts were first published in China Now, and in The Black Liberator. I am grateful to June Zaft for typing the final draft.
David Selbourne, August 1975

David Selbourne was born in London in 1937. Chiefly known hitherto as a playwright, whose work in the most recent past has been seen at the Edinburgh Festival Fringe, the Oval House Theatre, the Sheffield Crucible Theatre, The People's Theatre, Newcastle, the Roundhouse, the Dark and Light Theatre, Brixton, The Soho Theatre, The West Indian Student Centre, and the Traverse Theatre, Edinburgh, he is at present also Tutor in Political Theory at Ruskin College, Oxford, and current holder of an American Bevan Memorial Fellowship.

Stuart Hall was born in Kingston, Jamaica in 1932. He was educated there and in England. Formerly editor of the Universities and Left Review, and then of the New Left Review, he is currently Director of the Centre of Contemporary Cultural Studies at the University of Birmingham.

Charles Parker, BBC producer, folk singer, and winner of the Italia Prize for radio, created the Radio Ballads, in collaboration with Ewan McColl and Peggy Seeger. His large number of radio documentaries includes The Iron Box, on the life and death of George Jackson. He formed Banner, the political documentary and folk-theatre group, in 1974.

INTRODUCTION

There has been, at most, a handful of good and useful books by Western observers about China today; and few like this one. There are good reasons, both for the absence and for the quality and originality of David Selbourne's.

The Western World has never really known anything at all to speak of, about China, Chinese civilization, or Chinese history. The British were more familiar with Hong Kong Shanghai, and the coastal **entrepots,** than they were with the immense population and landmass, and the even more immense historical transformations of ancient, classical, and near-modern China. Under imperialism, the mind followed the flag, and where trade and the penetration of capital stopped, it stopped too. Beyond that was 'inscrutability' — that other world, outer darkness of signified ignorance, where only missionaries and the Hollywood musical do not fear to tread. This is part of the vast inattention, that collective amnesia, into which the Western mind has fallen in relation to those great tracts of the global history of people and places which belong somewhere other than the great plains and foothills of imperial Europe and continental North America.

The Long March, the communist revolution and the great proletarian transformations which followed, have only compounded that ignorance, deepened the 'inscrutability'. If we didn't comprehend the China of Confucius, the elders, feudal landlordism and the **literati**, China of the ideogram and the Heavenly Gate, what are we to make of the China of Red Guards and Chairman Mao, of callisthenics and commune and wall-poster, the China where no flies fly? It is simply beyond comprehension. That 'inscrutability' which was always historic and specific has become natural and universal. The ideological closure is complete.

Sympathetic Western travellers to communist China — other than those offshore watchers who hear and see everything with electronic eyes and ears, and comprehend nothing — have been all too aware of this structured ignorance. They have wanted to initiate a discovery, and to communicate it to others. Their mode of writing has therefore been appropriate to this task of primary learning, instruction and recovery: documentary in form, carefully descriptive, modestly analytic, noting visual impressions, anxious for completeness, for tests of representativeness, sceptical lest they be accused of being too credulous, of being 'taken in', scanning the newspapers and posters and slogans, trying by dint of accumulating just the right amount of facts and ordering impressions — faithfully transcribed — to catch unawares the immensity of their subject. Though the object of study was large, overwhelming, many of these observers, who had nothing to test impressions against except their own recording sensibilities, had to depend on that rhetoric whose test of accuracy and guarantee of truth was provided by the seeing and experiencing, the travelling 'I'. At its best, a mode of writing scrupulous in its verisimilitude: a documentary naturalism; a language capable of conveying the fidelity to observed and recorded 'reality'.

I don't want to sound knowing or smug about the best

work on proletarian China accomplished in this mode. In some cases, of course, it simply provided the cover for an unending scepticism in face of a historical movement tuned to a faster tempo, or, at any rate, a different tempo from that to which the West has accustomed itself. The truth is that this kind of never-ending scepticism, which often in our culture expresses itself in a rhetoric of weary and resigned 'realism', has no end, historically : no amount of travelling and observation and interviewing could ever shift it. It is the product, not of the world-weariness of the observing subject but the 'world-endingness' of the culture which has imprinted these modes of perceiving reality and history behind this 'I'. Nothing new will ever take place again inside this structure of perception. It is wedded inexorably to its own 'sense of an ending'.

Nevertheless, some kinds of 'realism' in the writing about modern China have adopted this rhetoric out of the best of possible motives. It is a rhetoric conceived in modesty; that modesty which arises when ancient eyes are cast over things decisively new, instinct with the antagonisms not of the past, but of the present and historic future. It is paradoxical; for it used to be China — ancient, inscrutable, China — which cast its ancient eyes of jade over our novelty, progress, restless movement. Now, it is the Western world which looks upon China with eyes as dead as steel, mute as pig-iron. It is the West, regarding China, which falls into silence. Reports conceived in line with this modesty have taught us a great deal. They have given us faithful-enough transcriptions of contemporary Chinese reality. They have lifted the veil, raised its shadow a degree or two. We need more, not less, of them; more, well done, and widely available.

Yet this cannot be the only mode of writing now about contemporary Chinese reality. For one thing, we know that this mode cannot contain or embrace the fullest imaginative response to the encounter with a new historical reality. It is too spare, too lean, too controlled. It deliberately distances the subject by setting, between itself and the object of its reconstruction, the veils of 'reality', of docu-

mentary truth. It submits to the overwhelming massive presence of what is 'out there'. But it has no equally dense internal codes, no equivalent intensification of the perceptive apparatus, no complex structuredness, inside, to match the reality it is attempting to appropriate. Before a complex historical reality as condensed as that of the great proletarian transformation of a quarter of the world's population, the single 'mechanical' eye is simply not a powerful enough instrument. It is — in the full sense — technically underdeveloped.

The fact is that, in spite of the immense richness of detail which is there to be seen, the structures and processes which have brought the Chinese masses to their 'present', and which are bearing them to a future different in every respect from that which now confronts Western civilization, are not — cannot be — visible to the 'naked eye'; for, to the 'naked eye', both history and the future are resumed, merely, under the disguise of present appearances. To get behind the immediacy of those appearances, to discover the inner structure of this great historic movement, we need a change of focus, a switch of lens, a mode of writing which does not "stick to appearances", which is not transfixed by the naturalistic illusion. We need a kind of writing which is 'scientific', not in the normal positivistic sense, but in its mode of operation; "all science would be superfluous, if the outward appearance and the essence of things directly coincided", Marx reminded us. The "apparent motions of the heavenly bodies are not intelligible to any but him who is acquainted with their real motions, motions which are not directly perceptible to the senses". What we need most urgently, is not a 'naturalism', but an 'astronomy' of contemporary China.

Paradoxically, naturalism and realistic fidelity have come to be among the few active modes of writing left to Western intellectuals, because such modes alone seem to hold out the promise that the subjectivism which has so often passed for 'the fully imaginative response' can, at least, be tempered and held at bay, if not actually deconstructed. That entangle-

ment of subject and object, of impression and emotion, which provides the support for 'fine writing', is an epistemological error which only an imperialising culture can make. It mistakes the subject of the discourse — the 'author' — with the account; in its imperialising mission, it believes that everything in the objective world must already be finished and complete, perfectly reflected in every twist and turn of the sensitive recording mechanism of the 'speaking subject'. It collapses the world and the psyche. That is part of the basis of what Walter Benjamin called, its 'aura', its nature as a magical practice. But it is also true that that kind of 'documentary realism', which turns the paradigm inside out — 'there is nothing in here except the hard, resistent matter of objective reality' — also constitutes its own aura and magic: the 'magic' of the real. Here a false objectivism replaces a false subjectivism, by a simple inversion. Here, style has not been transcended and transformed; it has simply been magically wished away, out of sight. It is still there, but we can no longer see it. It has disappeared into its 'object'. It is there, but "standing on its head". This is the rhetoric of a vulgar materialism.

Naturalism, for the Western writer today, generates its own peculiar species of 'magic'. It was not necessarily always the case. In that moment when the transformation of the Western world coincided with the heroic emergence of the bourgeoisie, shattering tradition and everything else in its wake, there was indeed a kind of 'realism' which cut into reality, even as it appeared most to be reproducing it. But, far from that being the moment of the generation of a universal form and style, good for anything and everyone, forever, it was a quite concrete and specific conjuncture; and its moment is over. "The manner in which human sense perception is organized, the medium in which it is accomplished, is determined not only by nature, but by historical circumstances as well". (Walter Benjamin, 'The Work of Art in the Age of Mechanical Reproduction', in **Illuminations**, Cape, 1970, p.224). And the factor which, above all, has produced these new ruptures and transformations in the mode of organization in the Western world is, without doubt, the irruption on to the plain of history of the labouring masses. It is this which has shattered tradition, and dispelled, or made redundant, the earlier forms of magic. "The adjustment of reality to the masses and of the masses to reality is a process of unlimited scope, as much for thinking as for perception". (ibid., p.225)

Two things above all, Benjamin suggests, follow from this. The first is the decentering of the subject. There is nothing wilful, or obscure, or simple about this. Once the masses enter directly into the transformation of history, society, and culture, it is not possible any longer to construct or appropriate the world as if reality issues in The World from the wholly individual person of the speaking, the uttering, subject. If men make history, but "under conditions not of their choosing", under determinate conditions, then the subject is, must be, fundamentally decentered. It is decentered in two senses. It is displaced from its Cartesian position at the centre of the historical process. But also, because that forces us to recognize the social nature of language, it also displaces the Cartesian speaker from the centre of the epistemological and signifying process. We are, as historical subjects and as speakers, 'spoken' by 'the others'. It is the end of a certain kind of Western innocence, as well as the birth-point of a new set of codes.

But, secondly, it has effects on the practice of transformation and appropriation — that 'writing' by which men and women produce a knowledge of the world, or sectors of historical reality, in language. Benjamin, once again, tries to capture the difference in his comparison between the magician and the surgeon. "The surgeon represents the polar opposite of the magician. The magician heals the sick person by the laying on of hands; the surgeon cuts into the patient's body. The magician maintains the natural distance between the patient and himself; though he reduces it very slightly by the laying on of hands, he greatly increases it by virtue of his authority. The surgeon does exactly the reverse; he greatly diminishes the distance between himself and the patient, by penetrating into the patient's body, and increases it but little by the caution with which his hands move among the organs. In short, in contrast to the magician — who is still hidden in the medical pactitioner — the surgeon, at the decisive moment, abstains from facing the patient man to man; rather it is through the operation that he penetrates into him". (op. cit., p.235)

Something of this 'penetration' is commenced, so far as China is concerned, with David Selbourne's book. There is absolutely no question that, here, the full — not the constricted — apparatus of response has been fully exposed, in all its vulnerability, to the shattering experience of the Chinese resumption of history. There is no mistaking where he — a Western writer, shaped by that historical reality — is at: no magical disguise, no disappearing act into the 'object'. Yet fundamentally and irreversibly, the subject has been decentered by this confrontation. There is no integrated 'I' here, observing Chinese reality; it is dispersed by the continual shift of level and magnification, decomposed by the shifts of position. The compilation of these shifts of position are now the 'discourses' out of which contemporary China is reconstructed for us, in their antagonistic fullness, as a 'text'. There is no pretence that this is happening naturally. The mechanisms of selection, conjunction and montage, the active practice of mounting one experience on another, is positively shown. Let us not mistake this as a simple act of 'reproducing China for us', as it stands: complete, microcosmic. The practice of comprehension and, above all, of incomprehension, is perfectly plain in this text — the struggle of the 'author' to grasp, understand, fit together, make or construct sense. It is not a conjuring act; it is a practice — necessarily fragmentary, necessarily antagonistic, necessarily incomplete — of penetration; the penetration of the new stage of human civilization which the Chinese masses are struggling to effect. I do not wish to present this as everywhere a success, a 'masterpiece'. Masterpieces are finished, and therefore dead. I have said practically nothing of what this penetration reveals: I think the reader should undertake *this activity of reconstruction himself. I will say that, if one of the most momentous features of contemporary Chinese reality is the construction of a new culture, then few accounts which I have read can match this text in its penetration of precisely what this cultural revolution consists of, the absolute historical novelty in which its consists. "The piano is a Western musical instrument serving the bourgeois way of life. We should treat these things as we do our food, chewing it, and submitting it to our intestines, separating nutriment and waste-matter. Similarly with our culture" (p.30). There isn't the slightest chance that this is likely to be a comfortable experience for the Western reader.*

But I want to end not with the practice of reading but with the practice exemplified in the pages which follow, with the struggle commenced, with **writing**. *"The tendency", Benjamin remarked, "is the necessary but never sufficient condition of the organizational function of a work. The tendency also demands an exemplary, an indicative performance from the writer. . . The determinant factor is the exemplary character of a production that enables it, first, to lead other producers to this production, and secondly to present them with an improved apparatus for their use". It is the "effort to alienate the apparatus of production from the ruling class in favour of socialism, by improving it". I commend David Selbourne's 'improvement' to the active reader, the co-partner in his construction: I commend not the* **view**, *but the* **eye** *he 'turns to China'.*

Stuart Hall
Birmingham, August 1975

1

In the early Easter-morning press of black-clad peasant-poor, slowly surging, scurrying and running (Easter-resurrection) crowds, darkened and disordered by strain; pushing and scrambling to the Hong Kong train for China, backs bearing down under shoulder-loaded crosses of bending bamboo, arms are extended, and wound taut, and straining; fingers clamped and clenched around pole-ends, or (older) gnarled and knotted to cloth-wrapped bundles, and suspended bulging loads.

Some are standing in stress, as if crucified (and silenced by the fear of frontiers), swaying and oppressed by noise, passing packed, station-by-station along the line to nearing-China, crowding home to ancestral China villages, bound, intent, to celebrate (with grave-offerings and magic packages) the Easter ghosts and phantoms of the unrisen, unrising, family-dead.

They are hedged-in, among incoherent, wedged, and wrapped baggage, bags of clothes and yellow-plastic buckets, black umbrellas and parcelled pots-and-pans, eyes setting and set in the sweating anxiety of carrying bags, cash and kids, unable to turn the head; passing without a glance their own corrugated-iron shacks, and litter (of blown paper-wrappings) on the line, passing by the turmoil of terraced-gardens, potted-plants, blue-hibiscus hedgerows, and apartment-blocks rising on the wooded mounds and slopes of surplus-riches (comfort-stations of the compradores), and scaffolded with bending bamboo; passing by their own slums of sampans, floating in the oily-rainbow water;

passing by buff dogs, browsing in the dirt and dried-grass of abandoned, stony vegetable patches;

passing waste-purple and waste-red slums of tropical, large-leafed dereliction, past disconsolate drowsing refugees, squatting straw-hatted, in black, under the awnings of squatter-shops, and shack-cafes;

past silent men, barefoot, walking with wooden buckets of water, shoulder-poled, or under black umbrellas on a dull dry day, up steep steps to their beaten tin-and-plank shack-shanty houses, by blossoming tender trees rooted in the sandy-red soil of this slum countryside, (the nearing, high, bare hills of China, faintly seen, faintly green);

passing by a gunmetal-grey buffalo-calf, startling, haunch-deep, standing alone in muddy water; passing shack-laundry and shack-tannery, sheets and skins drying and slowly dyeing, in the ramshackle, ghostly, fields; until all houses stop.

Cultivation stops. The border-fields are bare. Wild grass stirs in long waves. It is the closed area, between worlds. There is a waiting, watching, nailed silence in the train. An old, one-eyed woman, straining, shoulders her load, preparing for her descent.

2

Look, in a reception-lounge, a man in blue, alone, is lying full-length on a sofa reading, his shoes on the floor. Above, on the wall:

'LONG LIVE THE GREAT UNITY OF THE
PEOPLE OF THE WORLD!!'

You pass green PLA girls, set in grey space on a colonnaded terrace, slowly needling (in white face-masks, and with fine hands) into trembling arms;

you pass baggage heaped in a forecourt; you pass a white-plaster Mao in the station-courtyard;

you pass row on row of reception-rooms.

Sitting in a cool concrete room, light-green clean, and pastel-still, at a cold glass-topped table, you listen to the light, distant, tintinnabulation of the singing loudspeaker; watching idling cigarette smoke, lace anti-macassars, limp red flags, hot damp towels brought to the table; framed-Mao holding a cigarette (against steep, wooded, mountains); limpid, watery-green fields, through a window, and in water-colours on the wall; cups and saucers of tea clinking, you sit drinking in the cool, fan whirring, resting. A quiet, inexpressive, young girl, plait tied with white-beige wool, is painting, unhurried, the corridor wall, while you, (with your turbulent urgings, steeped and still clashing in the restless collision of persons, still sunk in that dark clamour and anarchy of souls and bodies, other self shunted into an iron-siding, a half-mile back, along the line), look over the balcony:

at the border village;

at young rice growing there in carefully-tended, light-green, watery fields, reflecting pale sky ;

at sitting, stilled silhouette-figures in black;

at a barefoot boy crossing the silent railway-line;

at grey-white-washed houses with dark tiles;

and at white letters on the blast of sixty-foot-long red :

'LONG LIVE THE GREAT UNITY OF THE PEOPLE OF THE WORLD!!'

Moving fast, the head turns dancing, buffeted from side to side (in desperation) at a boy riding a buffalo's back, ploughing; at a small girl, gathering weeds in a wicker-basket, a little child beside her crouching and quiet; at a young boy plucking a pigeon, the feathers floating slowly in the stream.

Under lichee-trees, (moving fast), a woman in black squats on her haunches, washing clothes; two boys lead the simple geese past the banana-trees, men in blue carrying water hanging from poles, in balance. Buffalo, goats, pigs, hens forage along the straight, narrow banks between the geometrical fields; dusty women, loading bales of cotton onto handcarts, hitch their trousers, turning their backs. The eye rolls, moving fast, over a dozen men pulling carts down an unmade road, starting wildly at a field of men, women, girls, boys, bending their backs, squatting, weeding, planting, and bending, hoeing in check shirts, trousers rolled to the knee.

In the train's steady speeding, to the sung 'East is Red' in metal chorus, the crescendo of hundreds makes thousands, and tens of thousands, poured into the peopled, crowded, fields, rhythm in movement for your drowning, flailing in the tidal wave of impression.

A girl-guard passes quickly down the gangway, holding a kettle, pouring tea-water; village and field moving fast, quickening into one, and gone, racing across main roads and into the city, past sudden, farmed, Canton-city fields and deep green, crowded, vegetable-plots, fringing factory-walls; past ex-colonial balconies and spinning swept-clean backyards, festooned with white blowing laundry, two minutes from the last-seen buffalo, standing dazed, stock-still, and hock-deep in mud.

Lost in the city, breathing slowly;

(in Hong Kong, roaming the blazoned streets of genital anguish and purchase);

in deep warm shadows, in the almost lampless night-dark;

watching;

listening to the slow silence of the streets, body vanishing into dark, peeping, peering;

listening to the slow steady brush-strokes of a woman sweeping clean, the slow-motion gathering-in of invisible clothes, and feet washing, in the village dark, at a splashing, spilling stand-tap, unseen;

...moving on, beside the sauntering couples, easy and open as they walk, listening to the soft concordance of warm night voices, the last tiny, tinny tinklings of bicycle-bells ringing, the splash and squeak of cycle-tyres on midnight lake-black asphalt, and the tired creaking of a last cart, heading home;

...in the little light streaming from a late cafe, watching the drawn faces patiently waiting, buying bowls of rice-food and eyeing it, silently, as it approaches;

(under the metallic arc-light, inking in huge darknesses above the dug-up, deserted, road, the sounds of slow, concentrated, men's-and-women's hard scrapings and crankings are of hand road-repairs; of bantering and joking men's-and-women's voices, made ghostly clear and resonant, by night and stillness;)

...watching the night-roadmenders' woodsmoke; burning, a white cloud rising fragrant into blackness, each rattle and shovel of gravel, each spade-clank on the metal rim of the brazier, stoking up for tar, a separate sound in the deepening silence...

walking on, down clean, quiet, sleeping alleys, (Hong Kong poor, bedding down in their teeming sewers and runnels, mashed in filth, *bolgie* of Dante's Hell, rat-ridden by whores and hustlers, avid for pricks and dollars), a peeping Tom looks into the last-lit houses of the people; triumphing over poverty, remaining poor.

5

You, passing, stop; night non-entity, moth-like, discrete particles of unmade, unstrung mind, all making for their quickening centre, lost properties of the mind homing-in, watch them, these last alley-doors wide open, set in still life, magnetic fields of force concentrated in silent rooms, in rosy, russet light.

(You have today seen a 'Lost-Found' cabinet, containing discarded matchboxes, mislaid combs with broken teeth,, travellers' crumpled cigarettes, old ball-point pens, lost-and-found keys, and small coins, set on a hotel's white cloth, behind hotel glass.)

In resonant, radiating, interior silence, you watch a man, in low-power lamplight, hand on cheek, reading late.

(You have today seen the street-slogan, saying: 'READ AND STUDY SERIOUSLY, AND HAVE A GOOD GRASP OF MARXISM!!!')

Outside, he can hear, looking up as you pause, a distant railway hooting, a tap running, and the soft footfall of a man-in-the-dark, passing, and pausing in the shadows. He is sitting at a small table in the centre of the wooden-raftered room, feet resting lightly on the bare, clean, worn, red-tiled floor.

(You have seen fine, dragon-green, ceramic litter-pots, touching them with a finger as you pass, set down on the pavements' edges, breakable, moveable, but unbroken, unstolen.)

Behind him, a high, dark-brown, wooden screen-partition, carved to the ceiling, wide as the room, a door set in it, ancient rood-screen, is icon-covered with red posters, roseate, blooming blood-red, small framed snapshots in red, clock ticking.

(You have seen, looking in its window for ten seconds, a second-hand clock shop, where all the second-hand clocks showed the time correctly.)

Along the old red-brick, clean, unplastered, unpainted, left-hand wall, are:

   a high-backed, long, carved wooden bench,
   dark polished with age;

   shelving with burnished pans;

   stacked bowls;

   storage jars;

   honed knives;

and three chairs at a wooden eating-table, where two women, wife and grandmother, are softly talking, dandling a silent baby; one chair free, set for Elijah, hungering.

(You have seen people in the streets, passing, eating from bowls of rice, as they go.)

Against the partition is a small cabinet, set with cups and saucers arranged on a white cloth, behind glass; along the right-hand, red-brick, wall are:

a sewing machine;

a deckchair;

a nest of carefully stacked, enamel washing-bowls, set on a red-tile ground;

a bicycle standing upright, on its own props;

and a tiered bunk-bed, covered with a clean white awning, draped to the red-brown, beamed, ceiling.

The family name is on the door. It stands open before you. The man stirs, turning the fingered page.

Passing later, the door is closed, the lights out, latticed windows opened to the alley, the sounds those of sleeping-breathing in the dark; minds closing to a fixed point of stillness.

6

Hung Da, teacher; in torrents of words (beneath gilt-framed portraits of Marx and Mao), says,

> "In the old days, the student would write
> that palm-leaves were like the necklace of
> a noble lady. He would write of the ornaments
> in his teacher's home."

The dull, vague, morning is ablaze with brazen-red trumpet blasts, and fierce totem-slogans, vast hoardings roaring a political awakening at dawn, to the daily war of millions with nature;

('THE ENEMY WILL NOT PERISH OF HIMSELF!!')

Cycling crowds pedalling slowly in state to work, Hung Da says,

> "Only by working among workers and
> peasants in the fields and factories, in
> colleges held in the doorways of the masses,
> can the student serve the people, and
> achieve a harvest politically and educationally,"

men, struggling, heaving heavy carts, leather straps cutting deep into shoulders, fraying sweating shirts into grey tatters;

('THE THREE PEOPLES OF INDO-CHINA
WILL WIN! AMERICAN IMPERIALISM WILL
BE DEFEATED!!')

Hung Da, teacher, says,

"Chairman Mao teaches that we should put
proletarian politics in command, combine
theory and practice, and teaching with
scientific research and physical labour in
production. Education must be combined
with productive labour, just as men must
walk on two legs",

dancing children pavement-skipping between cat's-cradle
strings, strung between the white-washed boles of trees;

Hung Da says,

"As soon as the students enter the door...

('LONG LIVE THE GREAT GLORIOUS AND
CORRECT COMMUNIST PARTY OF CHINA!!')

...We guide them to study the works of
Marxist-Leninist Mao Tse-Tung Thought, to
foster the idea that teachers teach for the
revolution, and students study for the
revolution",

an old man hawking up phlegm, and stubbing it out with a
wriggling smear of the toe;

Hung Da says,

"But the main problem in education is
always the teacher, not the student. In
the old days, the students were regarded
as the enemy. Teachers gave students
obscure problems, not knowledge urgently
needed. Armed with examinations, teachers
ambushed their students in sudden attacks,
and did not teach them to understand what
they had learned. So teachers, too, must go

out to the people to receive political education, and to re-learn their vocations",

glimpsing girls, rapt in a hall entrance-way, who run away
giggling, when startled eyes meet.

7

In the chalk-dust concrete air, grey metal frame-windows
let in grey skylight. Under six barrack-bare lightbulbs, the
class, coiled and boxed into ink-brown desks, worn too small
by years of occupation, ready to rise to an answer, leafs
through the wafers of the rice-paper thin text-book pages, the
room rustling.

Coming in through the doorway, fiddling with words, you
close up to the teacher's blue jacket, her pale face fluttered
with effort, blackboard blazing with hieroglyphs, ('THE BEST
WAY OF LEARNING WRITING IS THROUGH PHYSICAL
LABOUR!'), hands dove-tailing together, the class, breaths
bursting, applauding the greeting's brief moment.

8

Half-a-dozen veterinary hands;

    ('THUS KNOWLEDGE IS LEARNED FROM
    PRACTICE, THUS KNOWLEDGE IS RECOGNIZED
    IN PRACTICE!')

wresting, wrestle him trumpeting to ground;

touching, feeling, holding his bristling, palpitating body;

('LIU SHAO-CHI AND HIS RENEGADES,
TAKING THE ROAD TO CAPITALISM,
WERE DASHED DOWN AND DEFEATED
BY THE WAY OF PRODUCTIVE LABOUR
AND PRACTICE!!')

bared under-belly skin, bulging tight as a toad's;

('UNDER THE LEADERSHIP OF MAO TSE-TUNG
THOUGHT, STUDENTS, WORKERS AND PEASANTS
HAVE CARRIED OUT SERIOUS EDUCATIONAL
PRACTICE ALONG THE PROLETARIAN LINE!')

balloon-taut to burst in a bloody mass at a pin-prick;

('SINCE THE CULTURAL REVOLUTION, THE
THREE DIVORCES HAVE BEEN REPUDIATED
BETWEEN EDUCATION AND PRACTICE,
EDUCATION AND POLITICS, EDUCATION AND
PRODUCTIVE LABOUR!')

ripening for theory's puncturing into practice, nostrils quivering a thin snail-dribble into the dry dust, ears pricking at
shovels of dry red-brown trench-earth slipping, sliding from
shining metal;

('CROPS CANNOT BE GROWN ON THE BLACK-
BOARD!')

tugged and struggling girl-students' felt-sandals, digging in,
heel and toe scuffing the red sand;

('WHAT HAPPENS TO A STUDENT AFTER
GRADUATION DEPENDS ON THREE THINGS:
HIS POLITICS, HIS PHYSICAL HEALTH, HIS
KNOWLEDGE, PROLETARIAN POLITICS, NOT
MARKS, BEING IN COMMAND OF ALL
EDUCATION!')

a sick black pig's pink eye moistening, and watering slowly, into death-quiet staring at half-a-dozen hands, quickly preparing surgical spirit and needles.

In a sudden thrust, the nearing moment is stumped and smashed, wrenched hands holding on, eye fixating in silent squealing with pain of fear and effort, lashing his life into tatters, legs frotting and rubbing themselves into frenzy, trotters hoisting the ground away, spine squirming and turning, head heaving vertical and banging the ground into stars, ears flapping the earth and flopping still, tenderly held on his side on red ground, black pig on a red ground.

Beside student-fields of sweet potato, sugar-cane, and fat bamboo, medicinal herbs, millet, rice and maize, other girls crouch, with concentrated brows, and neatly-plaited hair;

('WE DID NOT STUDY MARXIST-LENINIST-MAO TSE-TUNG THOUGHT WELL, AND HAD MANY PROBLEMS IN OUR WAY, IN IMPLEMENTING THE TEACHINGS OF CHAIRMAN MAO!')

here looking in a white enamel-dish at a pig's purple-pink heart-and-lung, conjoined, under the humid drooping trees, you are breathing-in the sweet, warm, aroma of palpated life; bleeding in a bowl.

9

Giant revolvings roll their vast dusk forces, wheeling in dark-blue waves, seething through unlit streets, and backwaters, of the teeming Pearl River, (blind bats, terrified to tangle with life, streaking round and around blue-black colonial riverfront-buildings, swooping into their own darkness), bells and tocsins clearing a passage for the huge mass-movement,

gigantic tidal power of tens of thousands of workers, streaming
through the damp, humid city, heading for the centre; pavements and whole streets rolling, roaring forward with their
buildings, your feet and legs, invisible to the waist, wading in
such dark, deep water, riding and bumping against shoulders
bearing you on, swimming close to close passions, afloat in a
sea of faces lit only by cupped, flaring matches, (the old sitting in darkness in deckchairs, smoking, with cards and checkers
at candlelit tables, or tea-drinking in backrooms, talking), en-
flaming for a moment a nose-bridge, an eyebrow, a forehead,
an armband; borne forward, buoyant, into steaming street-
cafes, into packed wooden work-shops, (windows bulging),
thronged full to their riverside doorways, pastrycooks, carpenters in white face-masks, arms plunged into flour, kneading pastry, arms plunged into sawdust, planing door-frames;
carried away to the river with crowds, on to plank-platforms
of ferry landing-stations, (see the girl behind the red-lettered
kiosk-glass of a green wooden ticket-booth, head down reading), awash with raw-smelling river-waves, launched rolling
and splashing by boats passing, low in the water, down-river,
churning ablaze in the dark with rows of lit windows, engines
pumping the silence, ploughing their furrows through moored
and bucking junk-boats; flotillas of cream night-soil carts,
passing in convoy to depots, shit cranked into the carts' tanks
from storage-pipes at the streets' ends; slowly floating you
safe out of the current along unknown and unknowable streets,
into eddies of pitch darkness, drifting by barefoot women,
eating as they walk, and streaming, running children, playing,
playacting, hiding their faces in clothes strung, hanging between trees, still drying, arms around each other's shoulders,
crouching, whispering, laughing in a tight circle; drifting by
smouldering fragrant woods, set in small heaps, and burning
into tiny mounds of sweet-smelling black ashes in the gutter,
drifting slowly by near-silent couples, sitting close under bany-
ans, by the river-side, shoulders touching; at last, beached and
immobile, watching a man parking his bicycle, sitting down
on a small stone-seat by the dark river, head on knees, resting.

In the distance, shell of the cupped ear drumming, you can still hear the muffled echoes of shifting, sea-changing, fathoms-deep class-formations, and the undulant tread of huge crowds, walking on water.

10

In the lightest lounge-fragrance of curling tea-steam, your eyes narrow to the small focus of the white-cotton threads, through bone-button eyelets, on her blue blouse-cuff at your elbow.

She, listening to the courtyard clashing with tambourines, (shattering like glass on the hands-and-knees of her bitter childhood), smiling gold to the crows'-foot eyelines, her hands folded firmly, and resting lightly on the starched-white cloth-covered table, says,

> "Before the revolution, women, like all
> women, were oppressed by husbands and
> superstition; as time goes by, the political
> and economic contribution of women will
> grow bigger";

or, she becomes a dark-haired, pale-faced daughter, growing silent, in dark-blue jacket, blouse-collar touching the rim of a black-wool jumper, at the V-neck;

and slowly recalling in the starched room her crippled foot-bound, home-bound mother, born to be bought-and-sold in the scything harvests of cash-crop children, in the old days, (are hens stalking around her clenched, fist-sized feet, peck-ing the grit of a country-yard, somewhere?), she warms her hands around the tea-mug.

Or, she says, sipping quickly, one hour of words past, the room creased and crumpling, face flowering in animation, spectacles shining,

> "The piano is a Western musical instrument
> serving the bourgeois way of life. We should
> treat these things as we do our food, chewing
> it, and submitting it to our intestines, separat-
> ing nutriment and waste-matter. Similarly with
> our culture",

bird-thin wrists, in blue, resting on the table-edge.

She says,

> "We must use historical materialism to
> estimate its merits, making the old serve
> the new, in the service of the people, com-
> bining Marxist-Leninism with the clear
> characteristics of our own culture",

lightly touching the white tea-mug lid, with a finger-tip.

She says,

> "And, as to foreign culture in general, it
> is good to absorb its merits, making foreign
> things serve China, absorbing it, as Chairman
> Mao teaches, with discrimination; to refuse
> to absorb anything from foreign culture is
> wrong; wholesale absorption is also wrong",

standing up, smiling, pouring tea as the pot passes, your mind slowly turning, turning over, to the tired trousered woman,

pale with effort, squatting down open-legged, turning the tap
on the road-menders' night-canister of tea, beneath the suspended arc-lights, yesterday, wood-smoke rising into darkness.

11

In a bus window, passing sequences of action, Canton city
passing and steadily sliding into Cantonese country:

a boy's blurred washing hands in an enamel bowl,
on the pavement;

rubbed clothes waiting to be seized again, scrubbed
and pounded again;

two old men sitting down together, one leaning back,
the other forward, talking through the re-arranging
lineaments of familiar movements, in friendship;

are water-coloured into a deep-flowing, gliding, slow-motion;

a walking girl smiling, (leaving the city), at the touch of a
girl-friend's arm at her waist, hip half-turning;

are gradually weighed down by humid warm air, to deceleration, a man coasting and slowing down to braking-point, lock-
ing his bike, key in the padlock clicking, and engaging, there
engaged, (leaving the city);

a man caught off-balance in his doorway, bracing himself,
setting his face and body for the moment of walkaway;

heavier clouds, blurred and bursting, forming into near-
stationary suspensions, (into the beginning countryside);

a small boy, tiny, disconsolate, tottering to a fall, clutching his green sheaf of vegetables in a fist, held by hands at the moment of falling;

a high-raised brown leg, poised and tensing, of a scrawny-thin man in a singlet, nervous for the feathery-quick shuttlecock, kicked from the next man, to be kicked at, being kicked at on impact, in kicked-up dust, to the next man, tensing;

a shouldered bamboo-pole, shifting on a shoulder, in a stacked woodyard, let go into equilibrium, there at the moment of riding into balance;

(in the country), a soldier, in green cap and jacket, uniform-trousers rolled to the knees, crouched and bending in paddy-field water, fingers pursed, readying for dipping in a splitting second, to break the surface with another quick, dripping, rice-planting;

until, arrested gesture and held movement (a brown pig, having run, his back at the down-tilt of the see-saw, bounding body, front legs up off the ground together, ready to bound down forward, tail curled, ears raised upwards by past motion)

stand together;

all at a standstill; in dead balance;

waiting in stasis, for rain, a chicken-eye's dry gaze fixed in thunder, darted in a stopped head, leg raised, foot's claws coiled, not uncoiling.

When the first rain spatters into water, bubbles prick, pock, the pond surface, draft animals cropping the wet aquarium-green grass, peasants walking in straw hats in the steaming, flowing downpour, the near, rounded, wooded hills, misting, cooling into a fluid distance.

After the rain, faint fresh bells ring the last trembling, pendant, rain-drops into a toppling fall from a window-sill.

The eye is excruciated to a razor's edge by the exact, clean, gleam of clarified light, sense sharpened and agonized, in a light head, by a thin, precise, smell of burning incense scrupulously clearing the air, as the steel needle, fine as a filament, pierces deeply into a child's delicate cheek;

(pig-tailed hair tied into three, small, plaited tufts, silk-ribboned into tremoring red bunches);

child's head resting sidelong on the wooden desk-top, the other children waiting in their desks, sitting upright, arms folded into their own seven-years-old silence.

A voice says,

"In the past, they were considered incurable.
The past fills us with great bitterness, for in
those days, the doctors never came to the poor
people, for the poor people had no money".

A voice says,

"Later, when they came with their stetho-
scopes, they told the mothers of such children, 'You cannot cure them', and they went
away again. So we did not know how to treat
them. They were taught through gesture only.
In the past, they could know single words only".

A voice says,

"After the revolution, experiments were
made in North China; army medical workers
did repeated experiments on their own bodies,
and on each other. Some of the experiments
on themselves made them dizzy, and unable
to eat".

A voice says,

"Through practice and hard work, they began
to master the techniques. A People's Liberation
Army team, made up of nurses, medical workers,
and ordinary workers, came here at the end of
1968, and began treatment. Most of the dumb
children co-operated. A few felt pain, and were
not willing".

The small child lies, as if to sleep, head aside on the desk-
top, cheek for the needle, and at the needle's very deepest
push, pushing deep down into the lucid, glaring, quick of the
nerve-ends of all feeling, her tiny index finger, raised waiting,
(listening), to signal pain or dumb discomfort, suddenly wrig-
gles in sensation, hearts breaking in terrible dumbness, the
bloodless needle extracted, pore-point of insertion dabbed
gently, the day's treatment over, passing on to the next child,
nurse-teacher talking quietly.

The child's swift glances are soundless voices, signalling
relief out of deafness, speech poised on the apex of a tiny
raised finger, trembling into vibration.

Opposite the deaf-mutes' school, a young woman stands silhouetted against faint sunlight; waiting by the roadside, (who is she?), with a brown chicken sitting on the palm of her hand, not stirring.

13

The eye crow-flies to a grove of trees in flower, (lichee-trees turning pink-and-russet, coming into a strange season), a sceptic's griefs taking wing direct from the shadows, where uncertain birds with blazing coal-black eyes perch in the gnarled and knotted branches, desperate beaks biting and leaf-ing through their own dark, flustered, feathers.

The new sun has warmed the poor room's bareness only into a half-life, watery sunlight shining on partition-walls of bamboo, covered with wrinkled, whitewashed paper; dull con-crete and light, fluctuating illumination and shadow.

A teacher says,

> "We are poor and blank. But Chairman Mao
> has said that on a blank sheet free from any
> blemish, the freshest and most beautiful
> characters can be painted. For a long time,
> the children did not speak; they were silent.
> Then they began to hear a little, but speaking
> was still beyond them.
>
> They had to practise for a month of
> struggle, to learn one sentence. Slowly the
> teachers began to teach them to talk
> a little to each other, began to teach them
> simple songs, and steps in dancing.

We have sought always that teachers
should master the techniques of treatment
themselves, combining teaching with treatment in the classroom. We have begun to
send children to ordinary schools, to continue their education.

But there are still questions and problems".

His veins are knotted on his hands' backs.

He says,

"There is relapsing of some children
after improvement, some children are
naughty and fight with each other, some
children have learned to speak, but the
teachers cannot understand them",

sun passing behind cloud, the room's concrete, whitewash,
and pale-green skirting, deadening down toneless.

He says, wrist-watch ticking,

"They no longer feel fear. When the
children felt pain, and were not willing,
we took care of them, for though we
are poor, we are rich in our children,
and must look after them. We helped
them, allaying their fears, by demon-
strations of the treatment, for if a child
knows what is to be done to him, and the
reasons, then he will be less fearful, in
our opinion".

The room fills with dumb children;

everyone begins dancing;

children's flutes crying and wailing;

and O, before you, all are bursting-out, singing, grace acting and dancing, the sun's face shining briefly in a clashing blaze of cymbals.

In the garden, gimlet-eyed stranger, you listen to the noise of children, (exercising in a thudding ground,) blackbirds coming home to roost, dumbstruck at the sound of children's voices; talking.

14

Such a searching, stunned, look as yours wakes at dawn, startling; now gazes at itself, mirrored in the glass of framed imprecations, glowing in the dark-brown lacquered hotel-halls,

> ('THE ENEMY WILL NOT PERISH OF HIMSELF
> NEITHER THE CHINESE REACTIONARIES, NOR
> THE AGGRESSIVE FORCES OF U.S. IMPERIALISM
> IN CHINA, WILL STEP DOWN FROM THE STAGE
> OF HISTORY OF THEIR OWN ACCORD!!')

opens into the grey-gloom of the early Canton-city morning, ranging along wet roads, and settles in reflection on the dazzling light of children, in long bright lines, passing, stepping over puddles, singing, to school; on mouths opening in pink O's, on dark darting eyes and glances, the small running in sandalled feet, to keep astride.

Who is the woman, over there, turning her head, now raising a breakfast dish into luminescence, across the street in the dark cafe, dissolving the dullness? And who the man, passing in the back of a truck, bouncing to work, hanging on, and so changing his grip, as to catch the eye, in this instant of passing?

And who is that man standing there, under the trees, at a breakfast-stall, eating and drinking (metal clinking on bottle-glass), sparrows watching his crumbs falling, at seven in the Chinese morning?

15

And, what of breaths held, cheeks rouged-purple, three-year-old children, in sunlight, ready too soon to act and sing, peeping-in, joyful, at the schoolroom doorway;

or, children playing on a heap of roadside sand; hands gritty with sand-grains;

Mother Sun speaking;

or, wiping your hands and face on a hot hand-towel, brought to the table, and tweezered to you, by a smiling, trousered, woman;

(Tung-Shan-district teacher, mother Sun speaking, banyan tree-leaves unstirring, mind's eye drifting);

or, the woman with-the-red-armband, settling her motherly bottom into a wicker-chair, on the crowded pavement, watching the milling children and bicycle-traffic, at home-time; she and you, watching the boy at the street-corner bicycle-station, with a pump at the bicycle-wheel, puffing air in, pump-end and fist catching, and twanging, the piano-wire wheel spokes;

the playground radiant with hopping and skipping and jump-
ing, glossy, black, ribboned-hair, shining;

the waitress, running out into the street with a left-behind
canvas-bag, calling, (Mother Sun speaking) a man turning,
approaching her, relief in her plump face, to find him;

or, women wiping their tired eyes, with towels; steaming pans,
bubbling, (under the bare light-bulbs), set on piles of banked-
up charcoal, food ladled by a girl in a white face-mask, only
the eyes to look at;

violins and mandolins, hanging from the low, brown-red, rafters of the old music-shop, deep in wood-shavings, men sitting
and talking slowly, in a perfume of rosewood and varnish;

or, the touch on the skin, of a warm towel; the bitter taste
of tea-leaves on the tongue; the black bristles (like splinters)
in the white glue-jissom, in the glue-pot, on the office-counter;

or, the man squatting to shit, leaving the low stall-door half-
open, clutching the door-top, straining eyes glazing over with
effort;

a girl raising her delicate open palm, a lost rubber-band in it,
seeking the loser;

(Mother Sun speaking)

or, the waitress bending and picking up a package, placed beneath the eater's chair, replacing it in his hands, as he eats, lest
he forget it, insisting;

and what of the children, carrying flags and wreaths for the
'martyrs of revolution', processing, singing, celebrating, holiday-
ing, others walking past them, in other directions, not looking,
the two files passing?

Mother Sun says,

> "When the children enter the children's
> garden, Not-To-Think-Of-Self is our teaching;
> always learning to give away their portion,
> and pay attention to other children."

Children are preparing baskets of posies, and yellow stream-
ers, proud cheeks pinked, and in lipstick.

She says,

> "If they have someone to look after them,
> then they go to their homes, each evening.
> Otherwise, they stay here all week, their
> parents working, if there are no old men,
> or women, in their houses."

There are minature green beds all in a row, in shuttered,
whitewashed bedrooms, mosquito nets and hanging awnings ;
small green sideboards, names lettering the tiny shelving.

She says,

> "We formerly paid insufficient attention to
> a class education, dealing only with clothing,
> eating and playing. During the Great Proletarian
> Cultural Revolution, we faced the workers,
> peasants and soldiers."

In their hair, are red flowers, of paper; and a small child nestled between her knees, hair patted with touchings.

She says,

> "We carried on the movement of criticism,
> struggle and teaching transformation. Now,
> we pay more attention and devotion to the
> people. Together, we have planted and man-
> ured the garden, and together do tasks of
> physical and manual labour."

Small children with yellow ribbons sit in green chairs, at green tables, folding plastic-bags and card-board boxes, mini-ature fingers fitting small packets of sewing-machine com-ponents into wicker-baskets, for factory-collection.

She says,

> "We take the small children to eliminate
> insects, and to carry water. We teach fifty
> characters in reading, and to sing 'The East
> Wind is Blowing', that 'THE PEOPLES DO
> NOT FEAR THE U.S., BUT THE U.S. FEARS
> THE PEOPLES!', taking care also of the
> health of the children of workers, peasants and
> soldiers, with games and dances, tugs-of-war,
> and gynmastics. But in our work, we have so
> many shortcomings, for as to the naughty
> children, we are not good at exercising our
> patience, and have not yet written our own
> textbooks for the children."

Cheeks bulging, and blown-red, hand-in-hand entering sing-

ing, children's fists are clenched for soldiers; dancing with
tin-pot guns, drums, and liliput-trumpets, marching with tiny
red spears, red-tasselled and dancing.

('WHO COMES TO SCHOOL EARLY SHOULD
PUT THE CHAIRS IN ORDER!!')

Among the sunflowers and garden sorghum, in red, orange,
yellow, and blue, tiny arms sprinkle water, tottering down
lines of plants growing, (finger-cymbals tinkling, and dancing),
filling their water-cans at a stand-tap, small bodies bending
and scooping from big buckets, hands wet and dripping, water
from their hands on your fingers (singing), motherly Sun, in
peasant straw-hat, waving; a barefoot boy in the roadway,
watching her waving.

17

Now, standing in such dark, as if suspended somewhere in
trees;

by a deserted pavillion, in deep bamboo, inhaling, exhaling
the narcotic-perfume of such a fragrance, head in such cool
air, (and blown light with passion), shoes in grass, far-away
below you;

ears and eyes, only, prick into a dense and stilled silence, mind
stopped at its centre, comb-crest in erection;

a cock, pulsating on a glistening, wet, path;

waiting, in the intense folding and bulging tumescence of a

city's trembling, before day-break;

now suddenly screams crowing into the stationary dark air;
dewed and tumid plants, heavy with cold globed jewels, com-
pressed into a gleaming, sudden, bursting, dripping onto your
touching fingers.

The first hesitant birds chirrup with quick invisible movements, in dark branches; they rustle the washed-out hibiscus
flower-petals into a slow free-falling, through greyness, setting
loose the dawning day towards morning.

These are the last moments of night, and the first light.

18

Sitting on a bench, alone, with your breath bated; flowers
occasionally gathering themselves on the branch, and falling
into a half-light, time slowly stirring forward; awaiting the
slow-motion of a city's waking, awaiting the first signs and
sounds, (of men and women in movement), there is only the
sound of yourself, with your breath bated, sitting on a bench,
waiting.

Later, somewhere, a gate is opened, a pail somewhere placed
gently to ground.

There is no footfall. Later, far away, comes the sigh of the
first traffic, on a damp road.

Along the path of your daydreaming, a man cycles slowly towards morning. He dismounts under the trees. The trees await the heat, dripping. He props his bicycle against a stone border there. He stands still, for a moment. He places his hands on his hips, waist flexing, very slowly turning.

He stands poised in mid-movement, the silence of birds chirping the air.

Later, far, furthest away, faintly on a loudspeaker, a girl's distant singing; later, the clacking of sandals approaches on the wet path, sandals slapping the ground and passing, a young woman in check-shirt and blue trousers, with long plaited hair, walking straight-backed, worker's canvas bag suspended from a shoulder, walking to work, feet slightly out-turned, taking short steps, not hurried, feet flat on the ground, and passing away.

Your shoes gleam wet from the grass.

Later, two girls walk quickly through the park, eating from bowls as they walk, mouths at the rim, scooping, chattering, scooping, chattering, and passing.

A little boy runs to a puffed, full stop. He turns round, panting; to wait for someone, approaching. He calls out, feet scuffing the ground. His mother joins him, takes his hand, talking, he turning and talking; both passing away around a corner. Later, a man cycles by, bell vibrated into a tinkling by the speed of his cycling, and empties his nostril, (with pinching fingers), and is gone, bell tinkling.

A bubbled gob of snot lies on the wet, black pathway, a
flower falling into broad daylight.

19

Tensing their muscles, tightening and straining;

> ('UNITE TO WIN STILL GREATER
> VICTORIES!!')

dragged wheels embedding in mud, a sheeting grey cloudburst
lashes down its drowning columns and walls of bucketed and
hurled water, falling onto lines of hand-heaved, creaking carts,
leaving the city; all struggled barefoot, and high-loaded, lurching forward into the teeming gulfs of blinding inundation,
bullocks and buffalo strung to ragged and twisted-wet hemp-
ropes; glistening-mud-buttocks ox-heavy, wet-black and wallowing dead-weight, in a shambles, heaving hips tugged in a
lumbering sideways-dancing and swaying;

smacked and slashed by shouted, ragged, voices, marooned
heads of beasts turn mooning, straw-hats, clutched straps,
bodies tattered and soaking into veils of rain, dissolving
water-logged into mud-and-gravel ground;

majestic men and women toiling in thunder, ('WORK HARD,
MAKE PROGRESS EVERY DAY!!'), faces streaming, straw-
mats laid on their backs, mottled and matted with wet, work
on in the flooding, flowing fields, fingers, hands, and forearms
planted in mud; squatting, kneeling and crouching, buttocks
steeped in water, one extended leg pulling them sidewise, still
squatting and planting the deluge, and shifting in crab-scurries;

boys running, heads garlanded and festooned to the ankles,
with broad, sheltering, palm-leaves and branches, torn (dripping) from trees and shrubs by the roadside, burst through tor-

rents, metamorphosed into moving bushes;

girls in capes, heads down in the downpour, splash through
gutter-rivers, sandals in hands, faces smudged, running and
blurring, the rain calming into a steady, heavy, falling.

In green-plastic raincoats, long down to the ground, children paddle in rain-pools; in rain-hats tied under the chin,
('PAY ATTENTION TO HEALTH!!'), soaked soldiers cycle
quickly, ('BE ON GUARD, DEFEND OUR MOTHERLAND!!'),
drenched capes draped over handlebars. A small girl, under
trees, loads a smaller girl onto her back, hitching her up, slipping, dripping, clutching her at the calves, hitching her up again,
and sets off, wobbling, into the wet.

In flat land, the rain is abating; nearing the deserted black-
tarmac lakes of outlying airport-runways, (weeds growing in
cracked concrete), you see helmeted firemen peering out
through the windows of a red fire-tender, parked in a watery
limbo, wind-screen wipers switching to-and-fro, clearing the
fine drizzle.

The sky is lightening, rain draining down dark gratings,
feet slicing on airport marble, a storm ebbing and flowing,
peasant-carts and voices moving along the roadway.

20

This might be a simpler place in which to lose your mind
and body, before flying.

For instance:

46

choose a plasticated air-lobby arm-chair,
(beside a statue, and a book-rack);

dull the senses down, into a feigning
that it is all familiar, while waiting
for an aeroplane to raise them into
another agitation;

put away for a while the politics of your
word-games, for a calmer, more selfish
condition;

repose now in the purely casual fears of
the practised man's flying;

permit the eye of the mind to close down
(into a void isolation), inverted upon the
exclusive, imported, ego, barely in action;

then, confine all feeling to the security of mere registration,
or passive acquisition, body's eye simply ranging the high,
echoing, wall-slogans, white letters on red surfaces; complac-
ent or guarded, awake or dormant; and idly read:

'WE WILL SERVE THE PEOPLE!!'

'UNITE TO WIN STILL GREATER VICTORIES!!'

'USE MAO-TSE-TUNG THOUGHT!!'

'THE PEOPLE AND THE PEOPLE ALONE ARE
THE MOTIVE-FORCE OF THE MAKING OF
WORLD-HISTORY!!'

'THE DICTATORSHIP OF THE PROLETARIAT

IS NOT THE END OF THE CLASS-STRUGGLE,
BUT ITS CONTINUATION IN NEW FORMS!!'

and so on.

Next, you can try to yawn here, eyes half-open (in a pretended vagueness, as at the well-known) upon dull green uniforms, caps and faces, sipping tea and reading papers; kitbags,
and so forth, in heaps, on the tiled, or rubberized, vacuum,
(not stirring to notice). There need be no tremor, nor arousal,
if you hold them all in a steady state, struck in the balance
between boredom and the ironic.

In any case, it seems as if this 'flight-indicator' is only a
blackboard-and-duster, and some anonymous army-girl, in
equipoised pigtails, chalking, (with a standard, lidded, tea-
mug, on her bare counter). There is no need here for the mind
to break into motion. Waiting would be better, null or sardonic,
the eye roving the room, excluding the music, looking without a murmur; perhaps sleeping.

You find a point of rest at "Snow"; blankly eyeing twenty
(or twenty-four) lines of marmoreal, polished feet of a Mao-
poem; fixed, multilingual, in white and flaming red, on the
marbled airport-wall; staring, unseeing.

But loudspeakers break upon the stifled sounds, the girl at
her counter mouthing into a microphone, duster-in-hand,
announcing (through the muffled gazing and dozing) goings
somewhere, dullness suddenly buffeted by soldiers stirring and
standing, folding papers, handling their bags — a poem? — for
a flight to the North.

Sleep-walking (or fearful of flying)...at a standstill, beside the wall of verses,...mind upon the dull bumpings of bodies... and then, lines on marble...

"I will tell you the scene, in that northern
land:
A thousand li are locked in ice,
And ten-thousand li of whirling snow.
On either side of the Great Wall,
One vastness is all you see.
From end to end of the frozen river,
You can no longer see the flowing yellow
water.
The winter mountains dance like silver
serpents,
The highlands rolling, elephantine,
As if, in their height, they could challenge
heaven.
O, but a sunny day is needed, stranger,
To see them in the red dress of summer,
Mantling the whiteness.
Such is the beauty of these rivers and
mountains,
So admired by heroes,
By emperors Wu-Ti, and Shih-Huang,
By emperors Tai-Tou, and Tai-Tsung.
But they lacked command of language, and
feeling,
And Genghiz Khan only knew how to bend
his bow,
And shoot at eagles.
All are dead and gone!
And today?
O, are there no men of passion?"...

...jostled awake by fleeting lines to the stranger passing, pressed by the passage of feet and bodies, you seize upon the progress of these flying feelings, breaking through bumping clouds and bursting into the air, wresting into words and meaning a sudden speeding moment; this fathoms-deep, sky-high, escalation.

21

('WHERE DO CORRECT IDEAS COME FROM?')

Rising over the long, neat, rectangle fields of pastel-grey, dark-green, bright-green, light-green, channelled with cream water, (where you can still see the flowing water), lightest yellow, and washed-out plum;

northwards over Kiangsi, and Hupei, and over the Yangtze;

over Hunan, and the Hwang-Ho, and over Hopei province;

poems and statements are framed in glass, buttoned to the padded fuselage with silver studs.

('THE PEOPLE WHO HAVE TRIUMPHED IN THEIR OWN COUNTRIES SHOULD HELP THOSE STILL STRUGGLING FOR LIBERATION. THIS IS OUR INTERNATIONAL DUTY!!')

These are no 'hostesses', nor 'stewards', but a young girl in a green uniform-jacket, plain blouse, red pullover, blue trousers, black sandals, and a boy of eighteen, buttoned to the neck (with large brown buttons in army-khaki).

They pass slowly to and fro, with darting glances, hands folded in front of them.

She gives you (uniform-sleeve moving up her arm, reaching across to you, baring a black-strap wrist-watch) an apple, a sweet, a pear, and,

Four Essays on Philosophy:

On Practice,

On Contradiction,

On The Correct Handling of Contradictions Among The People, and

Where Do Correct Ideas Come From?

She has rubber-bands at her plaits' ends.

The sun is shining through the windows, on sleeping faces. She draws the curtain, doing it quickly, moving away, avoiding your glances, faces-in-shade, sleepers-in-clouds, unknowing.

Descending out of the blue, the dead winter fields are clay-coloured, and the bare trees stand in yellow earth; descending over ash-grey fields and low dykes, as if hanging, or in suspension over leafless trees; descending to the dun ground's movements, a lake catching the sun, a wing casting its shadow; you see, at last, the fine wintry details, and the first faint-green of a new spring, lightly grounding, alighting;

('WHERE DO CORRECT IDEAS COME FROM? DO THEY DROP FROM THE SKIES? NO! ARE THEY INNATE IN THE MIND? NO!!')

and, alighted, in Peking, in vertical cold, walking.

22

He says,

"The weather is cold".

In a blue cap, he looks at his hand, as he smokes.

"We can learn from each other. We have no
beggars, everyone has food. Before, many
suffered. Some say the population is seven-
fifty million, others eight hundred. All have
enough food, and clothes. No one dies of
starvation. Today, the weather is cold. You
see, the quality of clothes may not be good,
but we can keep ourselves warm in winter.
There are changes in the lives of the people".

He takes his cap off, and places it on the table.

He says,

"When a man sees these changes, he must
find out why, he must ask himself the
reason. For, merely to see the changes
means perceptual knowledge only. A man
must raise it to the level of rational knowledge. In our opinion, perceptual knowledge is not very useful; only rational
knowledge is helpful. It is having a basis

from which a man can make comparisons
between past and present, for without
comparisons, he cannot find out change.
Then he will begin to understand".

He replaces his cap.

"Foreigners ask why people are always
smiling. They say 'The Chinese people
like smiling'. No, I say, you should
have seen them before liberation, and
asked the people then whether they
were happy, or not".

He poises the stub-end in his fingers, smoking it to the
last.

"After liberation, the people stood up,
and became masters of this country. See
more things; your impressions will become
deeper. Raise your own level of understanding".

He stubs out his cigarette.

"Ask yourself the reasons"

23

Marching along the grey pavement, green uniforms made
olive by cold and dusk-greyness, soldiers pass with gleaming

spades and shovels on their shoulders, in rifle positions, singing gusted, and blown by the wind down streets, wan and
slate-grey, in this fluctuating season (coal and coke in slag-
black heaps, tipped and heaped on the darkening pavements),
small grey trees, leafless, branches wizened by the past
winter's cold, worn to a cold, dusty, waiting for the blast of
summer.

By high, grey, gothic walls in old colonial suburbs, by old
mansion-doorways of burnished red-and-green paintwork,
enamelled and shining in the grey granite, crowds in padded-
coats and fur-collars are passing into the last hour of light;
old women, hunched and foot-bound, are moving slowly,
hobbling down gritty alleys, gnarled and held in the grey wind;
and, under a bus back-seat, lie tousled, wrung-out, dead-grey
mops (stiffened dry into rigor), bamboo-poles in a cluster,
resting on gloomy, bumping, metal.

A little girl with a red arm-band, ('LITTLE RED SOLDIER
OF THE REVOLUTION'), in the dulling, deadening-down
side-street of dark-brown, wooden, one-storey houses, fret-
worked and fringed with elaborate ornament, (these are dusty
bumpy-earth lanes, and passages, between the houses), is
skipping over elastic-strings, doubled between trees, straddling
and putting one foot on the elastic, holding it to the hard
ground; breaks off and waves to a stranger, passing: then sets
off with her dancing, getting weaving on her cat's-cradles,
tipping and pointing on her toes'-ends, heeling and toeing.

Four soldiers march, in single file, along the gutter, by
small, grey, one-storey shops, flimsy and green-shuttered, tiled
roofs cemented-over, weeds growing in the gutterings; infants,
swaddled and cocooned, coats quilted to the eyes, are wheeled (creaking home) in bamboo pram-trolleys, older brothers
and sisters clinging on, pushing and waddling, in woolen padded-

trousers, split wide at the rear, bare-moon back-sides toppling
forward on all fours, at the doorway, a tiny upside-down penis
suspended over the doorstep; and disappear, crawling into a
grey courtyard.

An old man, in wispy white beard, stands motionless within,
waiting.

A clear enough light shines in all such children, walking
from school, two-by-two in dozens, swinging their arms; or
girls in threes, arms linking, singing, faces shining (in thousands)
in the dusk, home-going, city; old men staring motionless, and
waiting, withdrawn into cold courtyards; old women in their
grey alleys, in gathering darkness, hobbling towards tomorrow's
turning into springtime, gnarled, and well-enough held, upright,
in the winter-spring wind, for this remembrance.

24

A square, dark-brown box of coal like a boot-black's box;
and, two small scoop-like shovels, for small coals, gleaming
grit, and brushed-up sweepings, blacked and charcoaled with
usage, (like an old oven's long-used irons, kept clean with
blacking), stand on the faded blue-tile, and old floral-ceramic
floor, worn away by a century's shufflings to the counters.

There is an old, unlit, stove, in the middle of the midnight-
open, late-lit shop, (light streaming out onto the dark pavement) cold metal to the touch, corrugated to the fingers'-ends,
with worn iron-writing and a forgotten foundry's code-number,
small flue-lids rusting into a baked red-brown, at the rims; a
grey-black stove-pipe, sooted and smoked to a dull-matt by
years of nineteenth-century winters, in a cold climate, rising

cold and black, and burrowing into the white-papered ceiling.

All forward movement is centred on a small purchase.

There is a steady necessity in all such motion at midnight,
in an unlit backstreet, (gaunt in darkness), of single-storeyed,
shuttered, houses, of bare-bulb light leaking through shutter-
gaps, or shining wanly through brown glass and green glass; of
sewing-machines whirring in cluttered workshops, of men and
women night-baking, clothes and hands floured.

Searching a candle, a ball of thread, a small torch, a flask,
a bag of cakes, a salt-fish, a singlet, a box of matches;

the shop full, and holding steady, in a dull tallow-yellow
silence;

sounds, only,

> of whisperings, at the clustered shelves of
> jars, bottles, tins, dishes, boxes and packets;
>
> of small-beer stirrings behind the counter;
>
> of the slow, elderly men, (wearing faded,
> and numbered, overalls), painstaking at their
> wrappings of utility-grey paper;
>
> of the abacus clicking;

and, with each muffled rope-soled entrance and exit, there
are soft swingings on old hinges, of flimsy, narrow, wood-
frame and small glass-paned doors, darkened, rubbed, worn
paintless, pushed and pulled at hands' and shoulders' height,

in years of passage to such a small commerce.

Outside, a pedicycle passes you, wandering in dark shutter-ed streets, a man in a straw-hat pedalling a wooden platform-on-wheels; on its straw matting, another man, cradling in his arms a small figure, in a thick padded-coat, sleeping; a pony pulling a high load of brushwood, a man holding a short whip, sitting by the cart-shafts, drowsing, pony plodding on; a shadowy shape on foot in the black street, passing, humping a large sack, looking in your face, as he passes.

25

On a cool (courtyard) morning, (standing in the Square of Heavenly Peace), so early and quiet as to be white in mid-air, the huge pastel-grey square's light and sound-waves hang in a misted, becalmed, stillness;

all sounds and figures placed in the linear perspective of vast geometries, a gigantic flagged, and fogged landscape.

But the dark-blue, and old-black, silhouette figures, separate-ly walking, make up no still-life in a dead centre; this is no period setting.

These movements start upon no piazza (beneath a camp-anile).

This is the ground of a giant's field of revolution, set square and symmetrical for the multiplication, contradiction and resolution of the arithmetic of millions.

Here banners blaze red with struggle, and proclamations
stretch across the sky; here is the Great Hall of The People;
and here, when voices no longer whiten into the silences of an
early morning, children, gathered in thousands at the wreathed
and flowered cenotaph of the Martyrs Of The Revolution,
sing no nursery-rhymes, nor doomed anthems, but the roaring-
dark Internationale, unsynchronized sound, (an echoing second
after the mass opening of mouths in chorus), rolling slowly
across a dusty-grey acreage of space, in the metal of loudspeakers.

The day passes into an overcast noon-light.

Here is the place (no more the Palace of Heavenly Vision,
no more the Forbidden City) of the declaration of the triumph
of an old world's ending, pronounced before the great, red-set,
terracotta Tien-An-Minh gateway, moored in a mammoth-grey
sky, anchored to the revolution, entrance to the despot-
emperors once-golden, and forbidding, city, a burnished and
tiered red-paper cut-out, of painted wood and faience, a
Noah's-ark, hung with lacquered-red Chinese lanterns.

Here, huge crowds, foreshortened by distance, the masses
of workers, peasants and soldiers,

('WE ARE STILL IN AN EXPERIMENTAL STAGE
OF STRUGGLE, CRITICISM, TRANSFORMATION;
BUT THE GENERAL ORIENTATION OF THE
REVOLUTION IS DETERMINED!!')

gather, posing for pictures, photographers hiding their heads
under black cloths, at standing mahogany cameras.

To see the old orgulous palaces, bronze beasts, dragons,

terraces, temples, seraglios and magnolia-gardens, of the fallen
imperial dynasties, (devourers of generations, in phantom,
suffering, epochs), distant strangers, dark Northern people
from far provinces of China, in long black sheepskin, saunter
high-headed, stiff-backed;

old women, with bound feet, hobbling up long, shallow stairs,
of the emperors' terraces;

flocks of tiny children, reined together with the white tapes
of their leading-strings, babies carried in back-pouches, and the
young, wheeled in bamboo-trolleys;

all roll, flocking, and flowing, over the balustraded and hump-
ed moat-bridges, and through the great iron-studded, heraldic,
red doors of the gateway, beneath the blazon of Mao-portraits,
raging insignia of a revolution;

and through gate upon gate, (into the innermost grey-walled
imperial courtyard), a blazing-red and purple-passage, set
against sky, to the bleeding and overturned past, seen, now:
fixed, mounted and framed, in pale, cold, sunlight.

26

'FOR A PERSON WHO SHUTS HIS EYES, STOPS
HIS EARS, AND TOTALLY CUTS HIMSELF OFF
FROM THE OBJECTIVE WORLD, THERE CAN
BE NO SUCH THING AS KNOWLEDGE!';

dark faces in fur-collars, or in coloured padded-coats, squatting on pavements with children, (trousers split for a quick shit
in the gutter), waiting for the shops to open.

'THE MOST RIDICULOUS PERSON IN THE

WORLD IS THE KNOW-ALL, WHO PICKS UP A
SMATTERING OF HEARSAY-KNOWLEDGE, AND
PROCLAIMS HIMSELF THE WORLD'S NUMBER
ONE AUTHORITY!';

houses and shops fronting the road; and in the side-alleys,
grey-brick, and grey-stone with tile-roofs; travelling towards
country, walls become dry-stone, poor ramshackle clusters of
buildings, home-made, as of squatters.

'THERE IS AN OLD CHINESE SAYING, "HOW
CAN YOU CATCH TIGER CUBS WITHOUT
ENTERING THE TIGERS' LAIR?!"';

horses, asses, mules, ponies, carts heading into the villages;

'THERE CAN BE NO KNOWLEDGE APART
FROM PRACTICE!';

trees bare, the earth pastel-grey, tinted by lightest brown,
desert-barren; dusty; flat.

'IF YOU WANT KNOWLEDGE YOU MUST
TAKE PART IN THE PRACTICE OF CHANGING
REALITY!';

dry-stone walls round grey-stone and mud-plastered houses;
straw-fencing; wood, wattle, lattice; wood-strip frames; paper
or glass windows;

'IF YOU WANT TO KNOW THE TASTE OF
A PEAR, YOU MUST CHANGE THE PEAR,
BY EATING IT YOURSELF — THERE CAN
BE NO KNOWLEDGE APART FROM PRACTICE!!';

small horses, ponies, donkeys drawing slow carts, straw-loaded,
the driver smoking a pipe, high on top of the straw a man

sleeping; a man on horseback, cold sun shining on the winter-blasted ground.

'MAN'S ACTIVITY IN PRODUCTION IS THE
MOST FUNDAMENTAL PRACTICAL ACTIVITY,
THE DETERMINANT OF ALL OTHERS!!';

soldiers working in the silent fields, guns standing, covered in white-sheeting and yellow bales of straw; and the poor, wattle, houses;

'WHOEVER WANTS TO KNOW A THING, HAS
NO WAY OF DOING SO, EXCEPT BY COMING
INTO CONTACT WITH IT, THAT IS, BY LIVING
AND PRACTISING IN ITS ENVIRONMENT!';

tiny black pigs, scavenging up and down brown earth-hillocks, by the roadsides.

'IF YOU WANT TO KNOW A CERTAIN THING,
OR A CERTAIN CLASS OF THINGS DIRECTLY,
YOU MUST PERSONALLY PARTICIPATE IN
THE PRACTICAL STRUGGLE TO CHANGE
REALITY!!';

cold, dry, desert-like stony earth, hard dun colours; motionless ground; barely a little green growth, the brightest colour that of yellow straw-fences.

'THE MOST IMPORTANT PROBLEM DOES NOT
LIE IN UNDERSTANDING THE LAWS OF THE
OBJECTIVE WORLD, AND THUS BEING ABLE
TO EXPLAIN IT, BUT IN APPLYING THE KNOW-
LEDGE OF THOSE LAWS, ACTIVELY TO CHANGE
THE WORLD!';

in the backs of trucks, women wrapped in quilted coats, fur collars, hands up their sleeves; some sleeping.

> 'THROUGH HIS ACTIVITY IN PRODUCTION,
> MAN ALSO GRADUALLY COMES TO UNDER-
> STAND, IN VARYING DEGREES, CERTAIN RE-
> LATIONS THAT EXIST BETWEEN MAN AND
> MAN!';

a man standing (to the top of his thighs) in a small pond, in pink waterproof, fishing in a hummocked desert, with a large slow-sweeping scoop-net;

> 'MAN'S SOCIAL PRACTICE ALONE IS THE
> CRITERION OF TRUTH OF HIS KNOWLEDGE
> OF THE EXTERNAL WORLD!!';

in four or five miles of unmade roads, and unreclaimed, sandy sandhill, scrub-ground, men digging.

> 'HUMAN KNOWLEDGE CAN IN NO WAY BE
> SEPARATED FROM PRACTICE!!';

bumping over deep cart-tracks; women carting, fields in the distance glimpsed growing; by axle-breaking force, bumped and cracked upright.

> 'THE TRUTH OF ANY KNOWLEDGE OR THEORY
> IS DETERMINED NOT BY SUBJECTIVE FEELINGS,
> BUT BY OBJECTIVE RESULTS IN SOCIAL
> PRACTICE!!';

men and women shouting a hoarse, dry, welcome, waiting in a waste-land, and standing in sand.

27

Beyond sand, fields; boots on a bright cold day padding in moon-dust, wind gusting, sand muffling the footfalls, 'ON PRACTICE, ON THE RELATION BETWEEN KNOWLEDGE AND PRACTICE, AND BETWEEN KNOWING AND DOING', wedged, crumpled in your pocket.

Men and women teachers are marching in from fields, with spades at their shoulders, clumping and clanking them to ground, metal dropping and thudding to dust, hands gripping handles; sound stopped in sand.

A brigade-leader, come from working, carting, digging, ditching, eye settled and steady, in blue cap, jacket and trousers, washes his hands in warm water, poured steaming (in the cold, whitewashed, concrete room) from a large metal jug into a white-enamel bowl, set upon a wrought-iron tripod, with a metal soap-container, and a folded handtowel.

He speaks at a long trestle-table, covered by a clean white cloth, hands folded, nails tended, speaking slowly, softly (sound of wind blowing, swirls of dust billowing down broad pathways, between the billets and farm-buildings), saying,

> "They may look down on physical labour and
> the working people, when they come to the
> cadre-school. They have to pick up the hoe,
> confront stones, manure and dirtiness, Chairman
> Mao teaching that cadres should go down in
> turn to do manual labour, go to the most
> difficult places, study again, with hard struggle,
> self-reliance, and plain living."

The low ceiling is papered and whitewashed; six bare bulbs down its centre; tea-aroma, in bareness.

"They are confronted with dirtiness and hardness, but, through physical labour, they remove their own looking-down, themselves, and see that physical labour created everything, and is therefore glorious. Only in these hard conditions, can they confront it, fearing no hardship."

The self's eye rears up out of the seated body, bolting, (feet on hard concrete), teachers' metal again striking the sandy ground, in a cold climax.

28

"At the beginning, this area was just sand. Here, there were no trees, houses, nor arable land. In a struggle, there are two ways only..."

Tsien-Binh: "I entered the city, and divorced myself from the masses, as head of the Western Municipal District. But, when I picked up the hoe, half my bureaucratic air was got rid of. I realized why I was divorced from physical labour, considering myself not an ordinary worker, but some kind of officer. Before, comrades called me Head of The District; now Old Tsien is what they call me. This was the problem solved by the cadre-school."

"...Submit or struggle with difficulties. There was nothing here. We came with tents. We had to build everything, and make our own tools and implements, step by step; slowly..."

Li Ting-Shih: (her face rosy): "I had to cover my nose formerly, when I saw the night-soil cart, in the city. When I came to the school, I saw that the middle and poor peasants in the commune see manure as treasure. I worked with them, in the cultivation of sweet-potatoes. I saw a woman commune-member who used her hands to break down the manure, and spread it on the sweet potatoes. I was afraid it would get on my clothes. They think it a treasure. There is a difference of only one Chinese character, between the words for manure, and treasure; but there was a big difference between my way of thinking, and that of the peasants."

"...The peasants were struggling to reclaim the land. We began to work with them. They gave us coaching in their methods of production..."

Li Ting-Shih: (hands folded): "It is not manure which is impure, but my idea of it. Now I transport manure here, pulling the cart against the strong wind. It is I who have changed. There is a change in my mind, in my mental

outlook. The feeling in my mind
comes close to the feeling of all
labouring people."

(laughing)   "They call her the Iron Girl"   (giggling)

  Slogan banners, strung between the billet buildings, slap
to and fro in the cold wind : 'LEARN SELF-RELIANCE!!' and,
'HARD WORKING DRAWS NEW PICTURES!!'

"...Now, in three years, we have:

two-thousand mu reclaimed of waste-land;

bumper harvests of   corn,
                     sorghum,
                     beans,
                     and millet;

rice fields;

vegetables: pumpkins,
                     turnips,
                     and carrots;

beasts: pig-breeding,
                     ducks,
                     chickens,
                     rabbits.

We make our own metal: barrels, drums,
and buckets, for carrying our water.

This struggle is the best method of
revolutionizing oneself, transforming the
person, and the objective world also;

working, eating, and studying together,
half-day work, half-day study; less study,
in the busy season..."

The rows of beds are covered in check sheets; green, blue,
red check; at the bed-heads, two folded quilt-blankets, covered
with a towel.

29

A woman stands up in a cold room, at the sewing machine,
and says,

"We can make revolution through frugality".

She fingers a blue workers' jacket nervously, smiling as she
speaks.

"The women mend the clothes; the men
mend the shoes".

Hu Yu-Sio: (pressed jacket, black plaits, blue
trousers); "I am twenty-seven years
old, a teacher in a primary school. I
personally applied to come here. I
have been here one month only. A
young girl like me formerly studied
merely in the city, and rarely went
into the country."

"...There is hard effort during study meetings.

No one sits on the bed, but on stools only. Every fortnight, a person can go home for a rest, if he wishes. Here, each person stays for six months to twelve months. There are thirteen-hundred persons. On the East side, dormitories for men, on the West side, for women."

Hu Yu-Sio: (white socks): "We pull the cart one hundred li, to transport mud from the river-bed; to improve the soil. At the beginning, I thought, since I was very young and healthy, that the physical labour would be easy. I took it lightly. At the beginning, I was full of energy, and kept close with the column, carting. After several tens of li, I was feeling tired. My two legs did not obey the control of my mind. Gradually, I could not keep pace with the others, the distance between myself and the others increasing; but if I tried to keep pace with the others, I became tired."

The wind buffets the bare branches of a small tree, outside the window. A woman blows a whistle; the hens come running for feed, whisked from a bucket.

Hu Yu-Sio: (black sandals): "I saw another was tired also. We stopped. The cold wind was blowing. I asked him, 'Are you tired?'. He answered, 'Yes, a little. But, we

must take the chance of this
struggle, seize the opportunity
to struggle with this problem.'
When I heard his words, I felt
somewhat ashamed. I realized
all the others were going forward,
I lagging behind. I found, in my
mind, the idea of Fearing-Physical-
Effort, though I am very young,
and healthy. The difference between myself, and the others,
was a difference in mind, not in
appearance; nor in my body."

They are singing,

'THE PEOPLE OF THE WORLD WILL CERTAINLY
WIN!!!'

The sun streams through the windows of their bare barn-
hall, lighting up the rouged faces of the musicians, (a shadow
across the cheek of a girl with a mandolin);

in their work-clothes, men and women are bending and stooping, planting and hoeing in work-dancing, to stringed instruments, the violin, the mandolin;

fierce and plangent flutes wailing, fists clenched, cymbals
clashing, and the tambourine;

lighting-up the side of the old, cold, black iron-stove, casting
long rectangular shafts of light across the grey beaten-earth
floor.

Outside, the leafless trees, and sun, shining on the grey-

tiled farm-buildings; inside, the spring of expression, the flute's
running, fluid as a scream, flowing, flowing; Hu Yu-Sio is singing, hands in animation blue, with cold.

30

"...It is necessary to temper onself through
physical effort, by study and labour to re-
ject the philosophy that physical labour
means punishment, and to determine to
change the situation, by using our empty
hands. It is the achievements in our minds
which are more important, even than production of grain itself..."

Wan Nai-Ho: (pushing back the bridge of his
                glasses with a finger): "I am forty
                years old, a middle-school teacher
                in Peking, teaching fifteen years. In
                Chinese, we have the saying, 'It is
                not necessary for scholars to go out.
                They know what happens in the
                world'."

   Grey walls; bamboo-and-straw fencing, sandy paths; sacks
of grain and fodder; flat lands, ploughed and dug fields; stockades of animals; ridges of irrigation, first growth showing. Beneath the beds, boxes of clothes. Outside, bamboo poles and
long wires; clothes hanging, flapping, drying.

Wan Nai-Ho: (worker's cap, pale-rimmed, strong-
                lensed glasses of a reading man, blue
                work-jacket, elbow resting on the

table-edge): "Formerly, when I gave lectures to students in the classroom, I could talk a lot, and felt very satisfied. I talked of the peasants, but I never laid touch on a plough."

"...We realize that we are ordinary workers, labouring people..."

Wan Nai-Ho: (pushing back the bridge of his glasses with a finger): "I realized that intellectuals did not know what happened in the world, and that I was not familiar with what I taught the students. I was divorced from the world of practice. I determined to go out of the narrow room of the school, into the broad rooms of society. I take mud from the fish-ponds, and cart it to the roadside. It is useful in ricefields. My hands, feet, and body may be covered with mud, but I can feel happy. In the past, when I walked on the narrow ridges, I was afraid that my shoes would smell, and get dirty. In the fields, we have sand-hills, and hollows. If we want to cultivate rice, we must level the land. Who else will do it, if not I? It is a hard job, using spades and carts; but when I see that the land is changed by the work of my own hands, I realize the power of the human being to

change nature. When I go back
to the school, this will be my
knowledge. It is an education for
a person to combat nature, to do
ordinary labour."

"...But this is still a new thing, a new thing
born in China. We are lacking in experience.
For instance, what is the proper length of
this education? In the course of productive labour, how is it possible to make the
maximum gains in production? We make
mistakes. Some of the cadres are not so
confident in overcoming their difficulties
about physical labour. We have many shortcomings..."

"I am just like a pupil in this cadre-school.
There are many things I should re-study."

"...And, how shall a man acquire knowledge?
Shall it be by passing through the three doors,
family-door, school-door, office-door; or with
his empty hands? This is the question."

In this silence, it is cold enough to see his breath, and hear
the sound of stunned and stifled marching-feet; in beaten dust,
singing.

"And how shall a man acquire knowledge?"

31

The whip of a smiling man, work-dancing on one leg, his
face rouged, hand-on-hips, lashes his make-believe horses,
bolting to market; other horses, beyond the doorway and
windows, over there, are browsing the ground, in a hair-raising
conjunction; the teacher, with his lips drawn back in a rictus,
clamped to his pen-top piccolo, (branches beating at the window), motions to and fro with his head, at his own whistling
music, in a vortex of blouses, and trousers, white scarves and
red flags waving, and streaming.

The whip of a smiling man, work-dancing on one leg, his
face rouged, cracks the recessing mind, (the nail smacked
squarely on the head), onto a cart-track, pitched out into
sand, propelled by a fierce, dry force; to bump again down
the road-way.

32

Forking up into a wicker-basket, (on a long-toothed rake),
the straw-flecked goblets of pony-droppings, a man stands
somewhere isolated in a windswept light, standing beside his
bicycle-wheeled cart, tilted onto its shafts, prospecting for
treasure;

scraping and raking along the sandy trackway, wicker-basket
set by the roadside, he bends alone, stooping in a long, careful
movement;

scooping, shaking, and panning the gravel and sand, through
the prongs' tooth-comb, straightening up, weighing the brown-
black shit-load on the teeth of the fork-end, pitch-forking and
tipping it, gingerly, into the basket;

standing gaunt in a blank wilderness, clouds lowering, lifting
arm and shoulder, and bending to spoon up on his rake another goblet, straw-flecked, the light windswept;

standing isolated by his cart, tilted on its shafts, scraping and
raking in the sandy trackways, wicker-basket set by the roadside, bending and stooping in long careful movements, stooping
and looking round, engulfed in the dust-clouds of a truck,
passing;

two men in a field, in a circle of watchers (broken off from
working), irons pitched down, and wicker standing, wrestling,
are caught in tight arm-holds, feet trampling and dancing the
ground, teeth clenched, clutching, grappling, struggling, prancing, and gripped, locked, panting, bursting with laughter;

slowly passing towards Peking, columns of pony-drawn carts,
(laden with wicker-panniers), slowly passing clusters of poor
stone-houses, plastered with dry mud, and flecked with straw;

vegetables, (spinach and onions), in small clusters of green,
laid out for sale, on beige beaten earth at the roadside; or,
nearing the City Gate, laid on the sloping, bicycle-wheeled,
backs of wooden hand-carts, shafts tilted to the ground,
stopped at the crowded street-corners;

children playing beside them, with an old rough rope, strands
frayed and hanging, four inside its tied hoop, in an eight-legged
dancing;

one small child, helped by another, pushing along a small, grey,
wooden, vegetable-box trolley, with wooden wheels, a third
small child riding on it, beside the hand-carts, shafts resting
tilted to the ground;

passing columns of carts, hauled, heavy-loaded to the city;

and, passing the old grey-walled City Gate, (burnished and faienced, glowing red, green, and purple in the light's grey ebbing), the dust suddenly whirls into billowing sandy gusts, rolling and swirling, looping and dancing around the clearing, at the gateway, the spring-wind sweeping over laden bicycle-wheeled carts, huddled crowds, and playing children, quilted backs turning from this choking.

All is stirring, and moving, blurred and overwhelmed by the dusk-brown eddyings of a dust-storm.

Perhaps these are the hard-labour shovellings of spades, dug and tossed-up into dry air, and falling in heavy slow-motion upon the city.

33

Out in the open, walking the bare streets before dawn, erect clear air sweeps the small trees clean. The eyes hurt, looking in grey half-light.

These are sharp contractions, in a doorway.

A thin flat disk, the faint dawn straining sleepless into day-light, climbs, slowly rising out of the dusty, bumpy ground, over grey concrete. Moving in the first dead light, a man puts a thin rod-stanchion into a grating metal socket, arm, shoulder and blue cap leaning under a bonnet, flicking a cold engine with a speckled feather-duster.

Perhaps it is day. A gleaming, yellow-grey, sun moves into a pearly, shot, sky. A man stands alone against concrete, yawning and dusting metal, feathers in tatters.

Grey branches' nodes, knots, all clarified nerve-ends and knuckles, burgeon, awaken in broadening daylight. Bruised (blue) finger-ends are swollen, with pent pink blossoms, blood-gouts bursting, under the skin.

These are the feelings of the displaced person, passing, walking on a spring morning.

The breeze suddenly leaps from some limbo, knocking over landmarks; rustling, (thudding feet approaching in padding unison, singing), the wind flutters the red pennants of buffeted children, marching to school, into a stiff, blown, motion.

Along garden walks, later, there are soldiers sitting, uni-formed, in the sun, by the lake, on small benches; crouching forward, reading, in the open early morning.

In a dark mahogany-room, there are polished plants, lino-leum-leaved, potted in deep-green tiled corners. At a long baize table, topped with a heavy cold slab of green-tinted glass, girls' light voices and faces, speckled by spring sunlight, shining through wood-carved shuttered windows, are gather-ing, blossoming and restless to speak.

The ornate university-doors close heavily on conversation.

Quickly arranging themselves, chairs scraping, coughing,
bright voices suddenly say, springing in the air,

> "Our transformation is just beginning. We
> are in high spirits",

laughing for a moment.

34

He speaks quickly, suave or beaming, in rimless glasses.

> "Here they created the leading servants
> of the Manchu dynasty; here, from the
> landlord classes, were fashioned lords,
> to rule over the labouring people."

There are three cuff-buttons, and concentric rims, at his old
man's wrist-bone: of a white shirt-cuff, a grey pullover-sleeve,
a black-jacket sleeve, at the table. A young army-girl student,
in a khaki-green jacket, sits beside him, hands between her
knees, placidly at the chair's edge.

> "Here, the teacher used to ask students to
> say 'Lord' to him, giving them only 'eyes right',
> and 'eyes left' instruction.
>
> (softly) Our main method is practice, second
> and highest stage in the process of cognition.
> Theory in the classroom, experiment in the
> laboratory, practice in the workshop.
>
> (smiling, lightly) Thus we can unite theory
> with practice."

His hands are folded, forefinger poised on the serrated, buzzed edge of his gold wrist-watch winder; a grey woollen scarf at his neck, delicate; pink-wired to a small plastic ear-plug, voice fading, and nasal with deafness.

(loudly) "We say, 'Study less, but better'. The ability to solve problems is more important. (plucking at his trouser-crease) Examinations check the success of the teachers' methods. We sum up our experience in the main square of the university. (cupping his ear) We have only been engaged in revolutionary education for a short time, so we are still at an early stage, and not doing our work well. (gathering himself to a climax) The main method is practice, remembering that the only purpose of the proletariat, in knowing the world, is to change it."

The crowded room (of caps and tunics) rustles and stirs, students, teachers, soldiers perching on sofa arms; the door re-opening for flasks of boiling tea-water, knees moving aside for the passage. Chou Pei-Yuan holds before him in a careful hand, (to catch a flying question), his deaf-aid, buttoned into a dark-green crocheted case, fastened with a small white button.

(sipping) "It is the teacher who is the main problem in education, not the student. We have cancelled the complicated and old courses. (smiling, gold teeth gleaming) The teacher formerly crammed knowledge into the students' minds, like cramming the Peking duck. (fading) To give students the whole of knowledge is not possible."

He is sipping tea, wrists resting loosely, slackly, at the table, imperturbable.

> (leaning forward) "We see that sometimes
> there are questions which the teachers can
> answer, sometimes the students. When neither
> knows the answer, it can be discussed between
> them. How to combine theory with practice
> is still unsolved, but through practice we will
> try to choose correctly."

He looks about the room, easing, his glasses catching the light. He slips his crocheted deaf-aid into his jacket-pocket, with pursed fingers. The Deputy-Chairman of the Revolutionary Committee of Peking University stands up, hand in pocket, the room standing.

When the doors open, he pauses in the doorway, among shadows and breezy voices, moving over the threshold into sun and cold wind, unruffled.

35

Cho Sho-Yinh's breathing is on your face, sitting by him, light moustache growing at a youth's lip, pale cheek and chin beardless.

He is sitting on his student bunk-bed in a small room, dressed in a blue work-jacket, and blue trousers.

Over his work-desk, a text fixed:

'STUDY LESS, BUT BETTER!'

In an interrupted note-book, a text written:

'UNLESS THE PROBLEM OF METHOD IS
SOLVED, TALK ABOUT THE TASK IS USELESS!'

Over his bunk-bed, a text tacked to the wall:

'WHAT IS WORK? WORK IS STRUGGLE!'

A woman-voiced loudspeaker speaks out in the wired and
budding branches:

'THE PRINCIPLES OF DILIGENCE AND
FRUGALITY SHOULD BE OBSERVED IN
EVERYTHING!'

His fur-cap on a hook, Cho Sho-Yinh, bus-factory worker,
elected to university by his workshop, speaks, reading from
his note-book:

"Idealism and metaphysics are the easiest thing
in the world, because people can talk as much
nonsense as they like, without having it tested
against reality..."

On his table, are notebooks, books, pamphlets ('ON PRAC-
TICE', and 'OPPOSE BOOK-WORSHIP') and sharpened pen-
cils. The window is shut against the tree-voices.

Cho Sho-Yinh says:

> "My family wandered the countryside,
> And had no land,
> Working for any landlord who would buy
> their labours.
> They lived like beasts, by the roadside.
> They journeyed through Tse-Hih county,
> Poor people.
> They all became beggars,
> My father and mother."

A friend takes his hand; places a hand on his knee for comfort.

> "We were no more than grass on the pavement.
> They sold one of my sisters for a handful of
> coins,
> So that they might not die in the roadway."

Muffled music plays in the branches, blood bursting under the skin, Cho Sho-Yinh's hand in another's, sitting on the bed before you; a small black shopping-bag, hanging on a nail, at the bedhead.

36

Students ('PAY ATTENTION TO INTONATION!') struggle with the grammar and enunciations of 'love', singular and plural. The dark, packed room is grey with effort.

The corridor echoes loud, with 'love', and 'loves', unison voices, in chorus; the target, a vowel-sound and sibilant, fifty mouths opening up for practice.

Love is balanced on lips, palates and tongue-tips.

Fung Chung-Yun; with her broad, stilled face, and folded
hands; grey strands in her hair, bound-back, and gripped; deep-
set eyes, and steady voice; says:

> "I belittled in my mind, and forgot, the
> bitter life of physical labour".

> (slightly smiling) "I did not know how to
> work in a factory, and did not wish to, and
> thus, I influenced the students uncritically
> with the values of ancient poetry".

> (pursing her lips) "For instance, Tu Fu;
> we can treasure the old poets and artists,
> but we must judge them by two aspects:
> their attitudes to the people, and the actual
> role they played in their lifetimes; what they
> said, but also what they did".

> "I went with the students to labour.
> (Mao-badge, on a grey-jacket) I went to
> the country-side, to learn the language of
> the people, their bitter memories. My
> mental outlook is changed. (grey trousers,
> black sandals) There, with them, is a
> greater richness".

In the library:

Gosse's Father & Son;

The Centuries' Poets: Pope to Keats;

One-Act Plays of Today;

The British Drama in Three Volumes
(1804), "presented by Miss Bayton,
1910";

Grigson's New Verse, dust-covered;

the wind freshening at the library-window.

A young girl says, (with khaki-green cap and long plaits, a
strong languorous voice, a red star, a khaki-green jacket, and
red-velvet tabs on her uniform-collar):

"I am the daughter of peasants from
Hunan Province. I was a red guard.
We rose to fight the bourgeois line.

The teachers were teaching us to
become the bourgeoisie's successors,
with fine writing about beauty.

Born after the liberation, would we
come to know how our parents lived,
with such an education?

Shall the educated be divorced from
the rest of the people?

Do you see how many millions of our
class-brothers and sisters in the world,
not liberated like our parents, live miserable lives, like my parents did?"

In a dark, packed room, (spittoon-buckets, half-filled with water, set along corridors), are pronouncing workers and soldiers:

> "Chinese-English, Lesson Four: 'He
> found a stone step missing. He found a
> stone step was missing'. Which is correct?
>
> Both are correct".

37

Tickets tight in the hands, children in the street clutching hold of each other, tumbling up steps, soldiers, slow old black-clad women, pushing and jousting, army-girls linking arms, students, workers in hundreds filing quickly upwards, bursting over the top-step, and toppling into the auditorium, electrified by the light and the roar of anticipation;

flags flying, arena-crowds massed, in steeply-rising blocks of clothing-colours, dark-blue, washed-out blue, olive-green, khaki-green, yellow-green, old-black;

ranks of soldiers keeping their caps on, rows of red stars, dark-brown fur-hats, gangways jammed with seat-searchers, tense with desperation, children (gripped with a fearful joy) in pink padded-coats, red-velvet jackets, in green, orange, brown trousers, in spotted, squared, checked patterns;

multiple ranging spotlights sweeping into their blinking eyes, crowds boiling and seething for the announcements;

peach-rouged girl, in a grey jacket and grey trousers, hair white-ribboned, in white socks and black dancing-pumps, purple-ruby smile in a fixture, miaows into a microphone, and bursts the mass into sound, light and movement;

running and hurtling, orange-faced acrobats, in a silk cascading, tumble head-over-rubbery-heels into the arena, twanged, trumpeted, fluted and clashed into movement, crowd roaring, girls in pink blouses, black aprons, orange ribbons, and green-silk trousers, juggling and balancing, small feet and hands dancing, breasts and thighs in a silk shimmering;

plates whirling and whirring, spinning and catching the dazzle of spotlights, vibrating and blurring on pole-ends, flapping and clattering into slow-motion, flicked and spun into a stationary rim, speeding into one dimension, to the hard edge of the flutes whistling-crescendo, applause slapping the darkness;

ears narrowing to the grunt of the strong-man, pyramids poised, trampling on his skull-cap, silk leg trembling to water, cymbals clashing, flutes leaping, all bounding and springing, feet thudding, turning and twisting, silk stretching over rumps and pubes, whips cracking, crowd bursting with laughter, heads shaking and nodding;

cymbals, vertically-flung, spinning, climb the air, falling slow to tumblers, catching and clashing them, bamboo-poles, (hanging with bells), arrowed streaming through air, bells jingling and tinkling;

magic, coming home to straw-hats, spun, caught, and balanced, wicker-baskets upended and poised on a forehead, vegetables, sweet-corn, full baskets of produce, trumpeted guns and fix-ed bayonets, spun, caught, thrown, fired, balanced, dropped in a tottering chaos, the crowd sighing;

eyes narrowing to lids, lifting on disappearances, to fingers pouched at the mouth for animal-noises, bleating, mooing, cooing, grunting, clucking and squawking, simplicity mounting to a climax of laughter;

(children stuffing their mouths with appalling excitement,
not daring to blink for missing a trick or something);

pressing on to the juggling apex of incredulity, a juggler, in
Mao-badge, appearing-and-disappearing, and suddenly, in dead
silence...,

...moment halted, by a cymbal; act stopped down to the last
clap; an egg; and the trembling silk of the hanging sleeve,
pushed back to the elbow, for a monkey-trick;

balancing the crowd on a finger-tip, plucking something larger-
and-larger from nothing, and nowhere, old people blinking
and anxious, the knowing sighing and groaning, and laughing;

and sitting back in satisfaction, children's eyes and mouths
open with wonder, lost in most magical dreams and fancies.

38

He sits on a bench in the park, smoking a cigarette, a canvas-
bag on the seat, by him. It is seven in the morning.

You watch, without other function.

You sit on the other side of the path, as if not watching, he
doing likewise.

Inhaling, he loses himself entirely.

Occasionally, the path of diffident, preoccupied, eyes inter-
sects.

He nodded (did he nod?) just before, a perceptible inclination;

perhaps not.

Passers-by on the path break the line of vision, and pass on.

The smoke curls into the bare branches above his bench, and is gone.

On the dusty ground, there are the ghosts of men standing poised at their morning-poses, and slow-motion stirrings, balancing and flexing, seeking to bring body and thought to a centre.

The early morning is a flux, sliding to the surface in grey sun-light, the day too early for arranging.

Under the trees, on the paths, by the benches, beside you, sudden strides and surges into prancing and swooping, rhyth-mic convulsions of leg-and-arm movements, are quickly brought to stillness and held gestures, a prance held in mid-air, on one leg, a hand fending off some unseen challenge.

In a quiet hallucination, two men are silently springing to a shuttlecock, flitting and feathering under the trees. There are women gossiping noiselessly at the next bench along the pathway, children marching to school in the distance to the sound of a loudhailer, and its echo.

A boy pulls on white gloves after standing motionless on his hands, back arching, and cycles off quickly.

There is no sound, except of exhaling, and of the heart-beating.

He gets up, shoulders his bag and goes, the scene dissolving, fleeting away beyond all recall, save this one.

39

An ass lies flat on its side in the thin sunlight, in silence, skin scarred and scabbed, (is it dead, or asleep?), strap light around its belly. The black hose-lip of his horse-penis touches dust. Carts process into the past, in columns, travelling across the plain, towards the toothed and jagged Western Mountains.

A mass of water, pouched in black skin, moves heavily on carts, bulging and floating, contained by skin, skin-tight. In his History of the Eastern Han Dynasty, ancient Pan-Ku, celebrated historian of the first century, wrote: 'Things that oppose each other, also complement each other'. A bound pig, roped onto a creaking handcart, tries to raise its head, failing.

There are soldiers in the delicately-greening field, amid dust, clustered and padded women raking small-stones at the road-side; pack-horses, loaded for a journey; small children, carrying a grey, caked-mud brick each, to men and women building, standing to their waists inside the half-risen walls of a house; in dust, mud-bricks, straw, sand, building.

Two women, sitting on the back of a pedicart, are pedalled forward, another man, grinning a toothless, bald, and bowing Mandarin-smile, pushing from behind into a wide dust-and-stone landscape, moving across stone and dust and dune, to the mountains.

'The interdependence of the contradictory
aspects, present in all things, and the struggle
between these aspects, determine the life of
all things, and push their development forward'
(*On Contradiction*, August 1947).

A man stands in a lake, on water, fishing from a wood-
platform; a boy on a roof, among clusters of old houses,
smooths mud on it, perching. There are dry-stone walls of
small, rounded, river-boulders, herds of sheep and goats cropping stony ground, children rooting for herbs, by the dusty
roadway. Against the dry foot-hills, crouched stone lions,
camels (standing, loaded for a journey), kneeling horses saddl-
ed, elephants smiling in stone grimaces, wait, stone-grey and
monumental; this is a long avenue and caravan of beasts and
painted gateways, to the seventeen tombs of the dust of Ming
emperors, set to stand and await a last judgement, in scrub-
land, and beside a dried river of boulders.

"There is nothing that does not contain
contradiction; without contradiction,
nothing would exist."

The leafless trees are in blossom.

40

'No one to set foot here; or be killed.
Try to steal; and be killed.
Enter without permits; and be beaten.
All horsemen must dismount at the painted
gateway.' (*14th century, A.D.*)

Jade belts, texts of ancient law, gold-tipped arrows, imperial account-books, the hieroglyph reckonings of a golden treasury; large-character wall-charts of the distribution of landownership, and estimates of per capita peasant-income.

> 'Without landlords, there would be no
> tenant-peasants; without tenant-peasants,
> there would be no landlords.'
> (*'On Contradiction'*, August 1937)

Gold and silver ingots, golden plates, golden sheaths for golden arrows, emperors' accoutrements, for death-journeys and deathly hunting-days beyond the marble tomb; hoarding-paintings of landlords' overseers, seizing (in curved, clawing, and scowling clutches) ragged slave-peasants, lashing them to the multi-coloured ground, for non-payment of rents and tithes to their golden pharaohs, in the old times.

> 'No contradictory aspect can exist in isolation.
> Without its opposite aspect, each loses the
> condition for its existence. It is so with all op-
> posites; in given conditions, on the one hand
> they are opposed to each other, and on the
> other, they are inter-connected, inter-penetrating,
> inter-permeating, and inter-dependent. This is the
> fundamental law of nature and of society; and,
> therefore, also, the fundamental law of thought.'
> (*On Contradiction*, August 1937)

Amid gold-pots and gold-pins, and the empresses' inlaid head-dresses of deep-blue and green jade, set with jewels; amid the filigree feathers, and milk-white pearl droplets (in a desert of scrub and sand and boulder, a crowd sitting on green wooden benches is sipping tea, in an oasis of green conifers, in a green shade, in dust, in pine-needles);

amid: solid-gold bowls;
       gold spoons;
       golden chopsticks;
       and golden drinking-vessels of the imperial households,
gold to the teeth, are regulations 'governing the whippings of
servants', pictorial diagrams, hanging above the display-cases
to catch the eye (proceeding from the perceptual to the rational), of golden heaps of coin, massed in payment for a princely
wedding.

    It would buy a cartoon-mountain of rice-sacks, for a poor
man's table.

        'The matter does not end with their depend-
        ence on each other for their existences. What
        is more important, is their transformation into
        each other.'
        (On Contradiction, August 1937)

    In juxtaposed setting: the emperors' close-fitting skull-cap
head-dress, of golden filigree, a golden network as fine as muslin, surmounted by rampant golden dragons, roaring; and, the
patched peasant-clothing of servants immured with their dead
masters, with wooden utensils for a humble journey, in waiting.

        'You see, by means of revolution, the pro-
        letariat, at one time the ruled, is transformed
        into the ruler; while the bourgeoisie, the erst-
        while ruler, is transformed into the ruled, and

changes its position to that of its opposite.'
(On Contradiction, August 1937)

Amongst the crowd, pressing down the grey-marble passage-ways, standing, staring, whispering, peering, he cranes up-wards, reading, breath hoar-frost-white in the deep, cold, vault-ed underground, beside the tombs of the emperors (and their empress-wives, annexed in side-chambers);

and, no jesuit, neatly says, tying the knot of a dialectical argu-ment,

> "The Royal Family oppressed the people.
> Now we come here for a class education.
> I am a carpenter from this province. The
> things are very beautiful. They should be
> cherished. We should cherish them. We think
> it a holiday, to see them. But the peasants
> here will never forget the class struggle of
> their poor forefathers, that their labour
> built this marble, this beauty, in those
> bitter times, for the princes who oppressed
> them."

He stands anxious to move closer to the tomb, below figures-of-cost, in silver, (multiple zero-circles lining the sign-board), for the transportation of stone, marble, and heavy timber, brought from distant provinces, to the building of this chamb-er. He stands, looking up at a hung painting: of canvas crafts-men, (carpenters, masons), building this tomb, carving (on canvas) the bas-relief lions on the great marble-doors of this entrance-way; standing in the entrance-way, his blue-jacketed arm's long shadow falls on the neck of the lion, as he gestures, speaking his mind in the echo.

And, then, the carpenter from this province, setting foot
lightly across the emperors' marble threshold, leaps nimbly
to a political conclusion, beyond contradiction, consulting the
ground-plan to discover his precise position, in the burial-
chamber of the kings of China.

41

Straight towards you, the old peasant walks down, goitred
at the neck, growing larger; down the steep paved slope of the
interior walk, between the battlements of the Great Wall, snak-
ing, ribboned and studded with square towers, over the mounting ridges, and along the contours of the great, rolling, hills;
gait rolling-giant on the incline, bald-head bronzed, teeth
smiling a broken, blackened, wizened old grimace.

The sun has climbed through the boulder-strewn, barren,
dusty scrub; up, through stone villages of poor mud-roof
houses, paper-latticed; through clay-coloured gateways, nich-
ed with heraldic beasts; over bare trees and pink blossom,
heaps of manure and brushwood, donkeys toiling upwards,
loaded with panniers; up, to the level of high rocks, breaking
open the smooth grey hillsides into outcrops, and turrets, of
pink granite, so bright as to pain the eyeball.

Feeling and sense gather (for the mind) the extremest elements, in drastic conjunction. At the long green tea-house,
there are hundreds sitting at tables, sipping tea, resting from
heights and thin air, in the shelter of a courtyard; blackened
teeth bearing down; each body rarefied into focus, a stirring
and bustling sharply defined in clarified light, a woman sitting
in the sun, her back against the wall of the first castellated
tower.

Impression (the faraway lake, a lucid-blue bruise) is brought to the acutest and most intense climax;

gusts of wind rolling in a clearing;

touching upon each letter of the carved and curved graffiti, in the stone of the Great Wall's terraces, snow shining on the jagged, black, teeth of mountain crags;

foothills, plain and lakes, mapped bright, in the thin air;

mountain sheep, distinct, picking their cautious way, cupped in hollows, cropping the short, grey-brown, spongy, springing grass.

A young girl, her black hair shining, the outline of her head clean as a shepherd's whistle in the mountains, summons the listening nerve of attention (object now held, light and bright, in the palm of the hand). She is carrying a hoe, and catching the sun in the eye, descends towards the valley, and the russet earth of spring-crops, beginning to grow in a milder season.

Distinct, (a thin running stream sparkling in the sun), the magpie, blue, black, white, standing clear in the sight, dipping its beak to drink, a being seized entire, as it is, before you, an atom beyond fission; a girl in black-velvet jacket, and blue trousers, body's pressure urging a pickaxe slowly into the soil, clods breaking loose, pickaxe piercing the eye, the soft rustle of falling dry earth imagined into an existence, beyond hearing; the peasant's face fronting you, heavy jowl, grey stubble and old-adam's apple, bearing downwards; men and women squatting in the lee of a stone wall, and smoking as they squat, talking; two children, by the roadside, blowing red balloons, cheeks bulging, breaths exploding into the air, are all exhilarations of bright clarified vision, beyond mistaking; and the old peasant, towering and fixed for a moment, in a clarity and calm to challenge the world, moving past, and downwards, out of sight.

42

The gathering-up of a great dangerous sigh, old woman weaver Yih Ah-Li sits on the bed's edge, black-felt slippered feet lightly feathering and stepping the ground, hands falling together.

> "When I was born my mother could not feed
> me. She had no milk to give. She had tuber-
> culosis. My father could not keep us living."

Brow puckering anxious into head-aching lines, she suddenly looks down in desperation, skin stretching tight and shining, in the dim bulblight, on the skull at the hair-line.

> "He had no money to cure her. He
> took her to the countryside."

Her daughter, flushing with unease, watches the hands plucking the counterpane. There is a smell of cooking from the kitchen, sounds of whispering, slippered feet on concrete, a pan placed on a stove, bicycle-bells ringing in the street.

> "When he came back, his job was gone.
> We had no money to bribe the foreman."

Her old back hoops forward, chest bunching and crumpling, bones of the bent spine ridging the thin jacket; ears, elbows, neck-nape, trembling grey bun of neat hair; knees pressing together in silence, legs tucked, and pressing back under the cold metal-rim of the bed-frame; lost in the grief blossoming to a blown rose in the half-hidden face, and withering, in the head raised.

"My mother died."

Cry of transfixed and silent Guernica, mouth closed, head drawn into a fist, old body trembling, hands wrenching, pulling and twisting; breaks, an old low-pitched long monotone moan, brushing and bristling heads and spines into freezing animal pity and horror, at such keeening.

"She had given birth to two children.
My younger sister was given away, to someone who had an inn.

I never saw her again.

I lost my sister.

I became a beggar."

A sob stopped, a sob bursting and closing into an old woman's soft and steady unpunctuated crying, a mother's sound.

"I was eight years old.
I went out to sell flowers.
I stood out all night long,
With hunger.

What we ate was like that eaten by dogs
and beasts.

When I was nine, I found work.
I was no higher than a shovel,
Standing on tiptoe, to reach the machine."

Her daughter listens in silence to her crying.

"I was weak.
I had the disease called typhus.
I had no shoes.
I was beaten with copper tubes,
When I fell asleep, working."

Crying hangs over the head.

"Because I had no mother,
I was bullied the most.
I had no schooling.
I lost my job, because I had the fever."

Crying stares the dark room in the face.

"When I was thirteen,
I became a silk weaver.
We wove silk, but walked in rags.
My father died.
I lived alone."

A dead weight, at the bed's edge.

"Later, I lived in a tiny room, with my
husband.
He had no job.
I worked for him, also.
Also, for the children.
We were very poor."

She holds the rail of the bed-end.

The small room with its bare swept floor, falls away, slowly falling.

43

On the bed, wrapped in green plastic, there are three, folded
up, padded-blankets. Behind her, a large wardrobe, showing
her back's reflection, and the thin nape of her neck below her
pinned-up grey hair. Stored on the wardrobe-top, a suitcase;
baskets, and a pan put-away, covered in white paper, and
bound with string. The door, doorway, and window-frame,
are painted green, walls whitewashed. A sewing-machine is
covered with a lace cloth; a newspaper's front-page is folded
back, half-read; a metal tray and glasses, covered with a purple
cloth, stand on a small table.

There are three small lacquered-red stools; a radio, with
a lace cloth on it, stands on a chest of drawers; also, a chiming-
clock showing the date, a feather-duster, two small light-blue
thin-necked vases; a framed photograph of herself, and, tucked
inside its frame, snapshots of her children; on the wall, a map
of the world; and light-blue cotton curtains at the window.
The bare floor is concrete.

She rests her hand on her cheek, staring, leaning her elbows
on the bed-end. Her hair is carefully brushed, and clipped with
one hair-grip. There is a long silence. On the wall, is a poster
of a soldier, peering into a dark night, dimly lit by the moon,
through deep grass.

"They wore smart clothes, and thought:
'You workers are coarse people'. They
even checked our pockets in the evening.
They thought that, without themselves,
the factories would stop working. They
thought that, without them, the world
would stop turning."

She folds her hands, to still them.

44

The room feels cold, a matter of swept concrete, and posters.

The neighbours' girls, gathered in the doorway to listen,
arms around each other, (for reassurance), hold her at the
bed's edge, under pressure. Puffed and flushed cheeks pluck
relief in brushing, smoothing, and composing the sleeves
of her jacket. The avoiding eye roams over her spectacle-case,
the open newspaper, the poster of a worker holding a red book,
snapshots of her children showing them as soldiers; and makes
a new addition.

She looks at her clasped hands, turning them from side to
side.

"In the old society, nobody took account of
what women said, only of the husband. First
the girl children relied on the parents; then
they relied on their husbands. That is why
they had no rights. They had to obey, or be
beaten."

There is a knot of arms, fingers, and plaits in the doorway,
more faces pressing to listen, small touchings and rapt whisperings to silence.

"We were treated like beasts; working in
factories, and doing the domestic work.
Now I lead a happy life,"

smoothing the counterpane into an apology for shortcomings.

"I look after the school-children who
come home before their parents, and
when they are ill also. All the parents
who are working need someone to look
after their children."

In the pause, there is a calendar on the wall, a small glass-
case containing animal ornaments, two glass-birds. There are
three shelves in the wardrobe.

"I compare this with the death from
misery and disease, of my mother."

The falling intonation skirts the edge of a weeping tone,
and steadies itself with a tremor and a sigh. The room's charg-

ed elements gather towards an ending. She says,

"I ask myself the reasons."

Heads crane more closely; latecomers in the corridor, asking questions, are silenced, a girl's arm, (an armband pinned to her sleeve, with a safety-pin), slowly passing glasses over heads, and through the doorway, to old Yih Ah-Li's kitchen, dark with cooking.

"We became masters of the country. If we had not learned that we are masters of all things, and that we can change nature with our empty hands, I think we should have died long ago."

The room settles in a steady state, beyond the word-monger. Someone says, "Yih Ah-Li suffered."

She stands up very small, jacket-sleeves too long, hands folded in front of her, by the bed, puffed cheeks sinking her eyes out of sight, in a wrinkled, relieved smiling, compounded of a child standing with flowers, a framed photograph of her younger face, a weaver's life, and three padded blankets, faded, and wrapped in green plastic.

45

Machines clanking and trampling ('MARKS ARE NOT THE LIFE-BLOOD OF THE STUDENT!') in a sudden blaze of black sunlight, acid-hot school-factory yard pungent and stinging, with acrid scrap-metal;

'We are still spreading knowledge as a duty,
but we must also educate people to be the
successors of the proletariat, and not to
seek fame and reward for themselves';

metal plates, drilling and grating the teeth's edge, cable-harness
machines whirling, weaving and winding around circuit-wires
of heavy-vehicle wiring-systems, and ears drummed by wheels,
milling and grinding in machine-oil ('TO LEARN·TECHNIQUE
IS NOT THE MAIN PURPOSE, BUT TO GET IN TOUCH
WITH PRACTICE!');

long lean-to work-sheds, old planking floors, windows set uneven, old transverse timbers papered and white-washed,
('BUILDING A SCHOOL-FACTORY IS THE SAME AS
BUILDING A GREAT COUNTRY!'), workers from machine-
tool factories and teachers at bench-work, stained and soiled
by spare-parts, black hammers, and oil-rags ('WE MUST
LEARN FROM EACH OTHER!');

black painted yard-walls, roofed against rain, purple-written
with chalk-texts of greeting and invocation;

'EDUCATION MUST SERVE THE PROLETARIAT!';

'STUDY ENGLISH FOR THE REVOLUTION!';

'A FOREIGN LANGUAGE IS A WEAPON IN
THE STRUGGLES OF LIFE!';

white dust blazing to a hot dry outburst, hard-baked sunlight
shining through small windows, on rolling-wet black metal;

an old man, with teachers youths and girls, in a machine-shop,
in blackened overalls, gnarled, bald, and scarred, saying,

"I was oppressed by capitalists, imperialists,
and Europeans, so I am duty bound to help
to teach the younger generation",

old scar-tissue around his lacerated, puckered mouth, and
scaly dry hand, blinking into the background, in the rattling
vibration;

quieter, bitter-chemical back-waters, of careful white coats,
plaits and armbands, engraving on metal, cameras on old iron-
tripods, ceramic vats and plastic circuit-plates, gelatine, mag-
nifying glasses, and mats in the doorway;

and a high sea of seventeen-hundred faces;

'If some children don't know why they are
studying, and think it is their parents who
are telling them; or, if they think they are
too young to work, and too old to play, so
therefore come to school, we have to help
them by telling them why they are studying,
to build socialism',

exercising in the sunblast, running pumps on dry earth, like
rain thundering a roof; a school-girl saying,

"I have a better mastery of cultural
knowledge, but do not pay enough
attention to theory. Sometimes I am
proud and sad. I am not very steady in
making progress, but have tried to use
the philosophical method of analysing-
a-point-in-two-ways. In the classroom,
I am not so active in answering questions, nor in physical training";

seventeen-hundred hips bending and seventeen-hundred pairs
of hands swing to their sides at the upright, in slapped sound-

waves, shimmering in heat, breaking and scattering; all the girls dancing and skipping.

All this sour perfume of metals (and hot hard-edged shadow) was set to black-braided girls' pinked and astringent singing, piercing voices rising somewhere in a turbulent crescendo, and flying, with quick darting looks, through metal.

46

The mufflings of Peking dust stifle and stop droning thought, in packed back-streets.

With a lost grip, unbalancing with effort, letting-go, his handcart slews round, wheels slurring the ground. Roped boxes and cases tilt, tottering, not falling.

Fur-collared overcoats, mounded in back-street shops, buzzing with sun and dust, glassed in old rose-wood show-cases, swarm dizzy with motionless large moth-balls, like sugar-coated almonds.

Four children, gauzy with scarves, pass cramped in a bamboo-cart, two sleeping, one gazing, one sucking at a feeding-bottle, in sleepy swallows.

Bald men squat under crowded awnings, sharpening knives, honing.

Massed heaps of coke stand, unloaded.

A dried pink carcass is grappled with hooks, and thrown in heaving motion, from piled carts-to-hands-to-trestle-tables.

Cobblers are near-dozing at their lasts, in dark and dreaming work. Dust flurries in a hot full wind, gritting the teeth and closing the smarting eyes.

"Face masks are for three purposes:

1. Against dust and dirt.

2. To keep nose and mouth warm.

3. To protect others if you have a cold or cough."

Straw flecks the swollen air, blown from dried droppings. A child, blinking against sunny whirls of wind, clutches a twig of pink blossom, passing and glancing.

A soldier, walking, puffs once on a cigarette-holder. An old squat woman selling ice-cream, leans against a wall in shade, smoking a pipe, stubbing the bowl with her thumb. Curved-concrete sections of air-raid shelters stack the sidewalks. Sun shines worn trousers. People pass through old, creaking, louvered shop-doors, faded flower-tiles swinging to-and-fro in them.

Dust blows the fuzzy brushwood, neaped, hauled by horses, drivers sitting under woven-matting awnings, whips laid on their knees, a stately swaying. An old man is pushed slowly along in an orange-box on wheels, squeaking and bumping around an unevenly-flagged corner.

Inside a silent courtyard, a boy sits on beaten earth;

in shadow;

making a box;

clothes hanging, unstirring;

beside a bicycle, earthenware pots, a leafless tree, and wicker-baskets;

O, all the dreaming, giddy strolling girls, sun-in-hair, in thronging, trundling, back-alleys of the filled city;

adrift, drowsy, leaving, losing sight of the seething city;

stepping on it, headlong in a bus, past the last man stripped to the waist, motionless beside a straw-plaited airport windbreak (is he working, is he sleeping?);

and, pulling up steep, through heavy hazy air, you fly at the red sun, riding, high, into a different province.

47

Alighting, in a yellow rape-field.

Breezy white goats are loose in fresh air, and bounding in grass, chased by boys, (left behind and trailing knee-deep in a wet green meadow). Fragrant and pink peach-blossom stands in shrubbery-green rain. Here is a garden-green spring-time, dust-laid, of sowing.

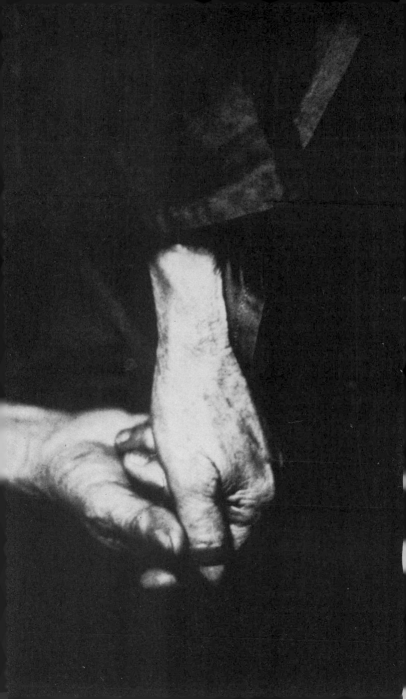

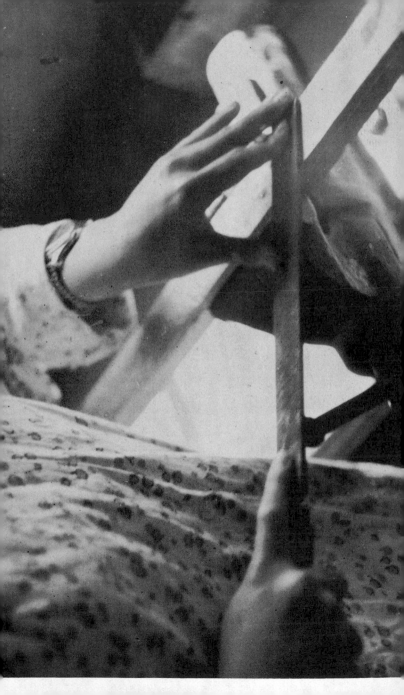

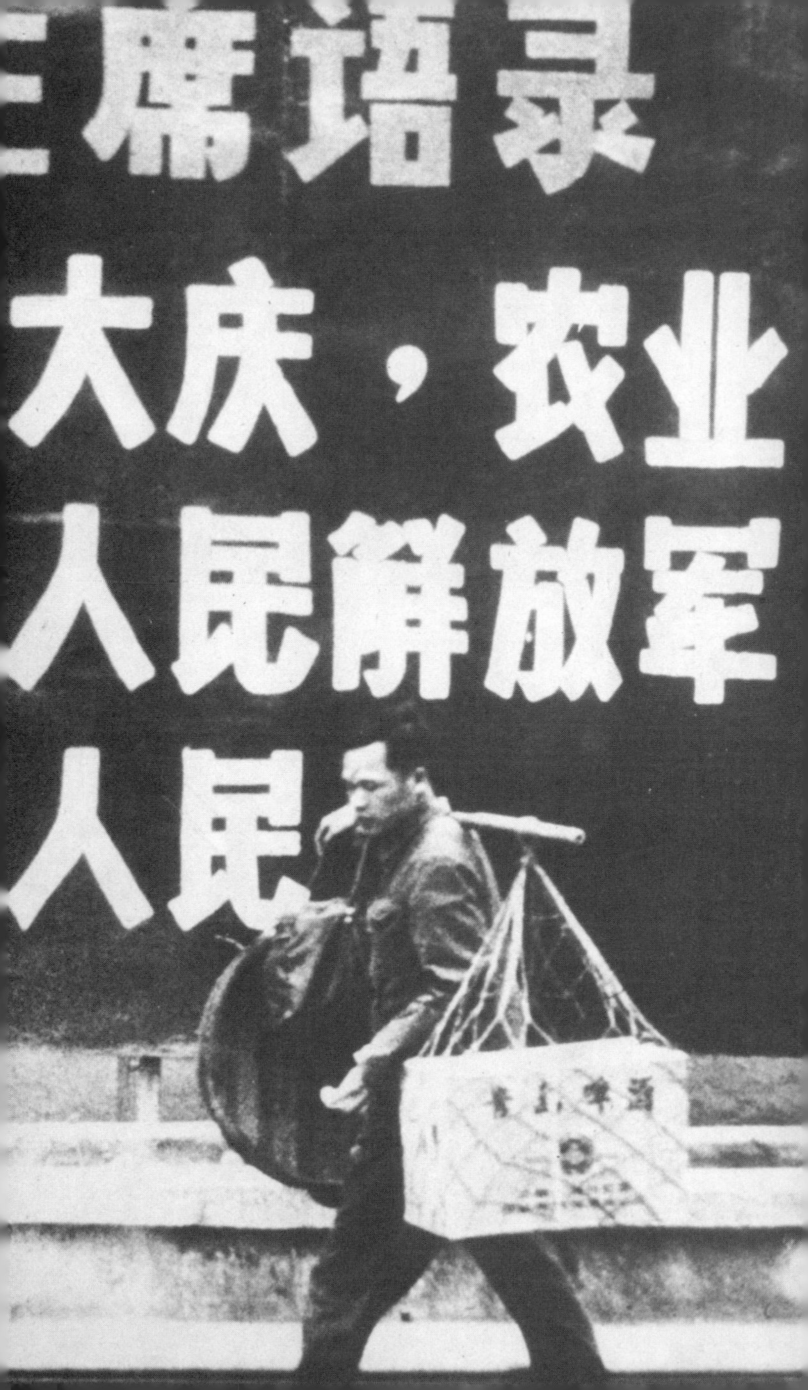

席语录
大庆，农业
人民解放军
人民

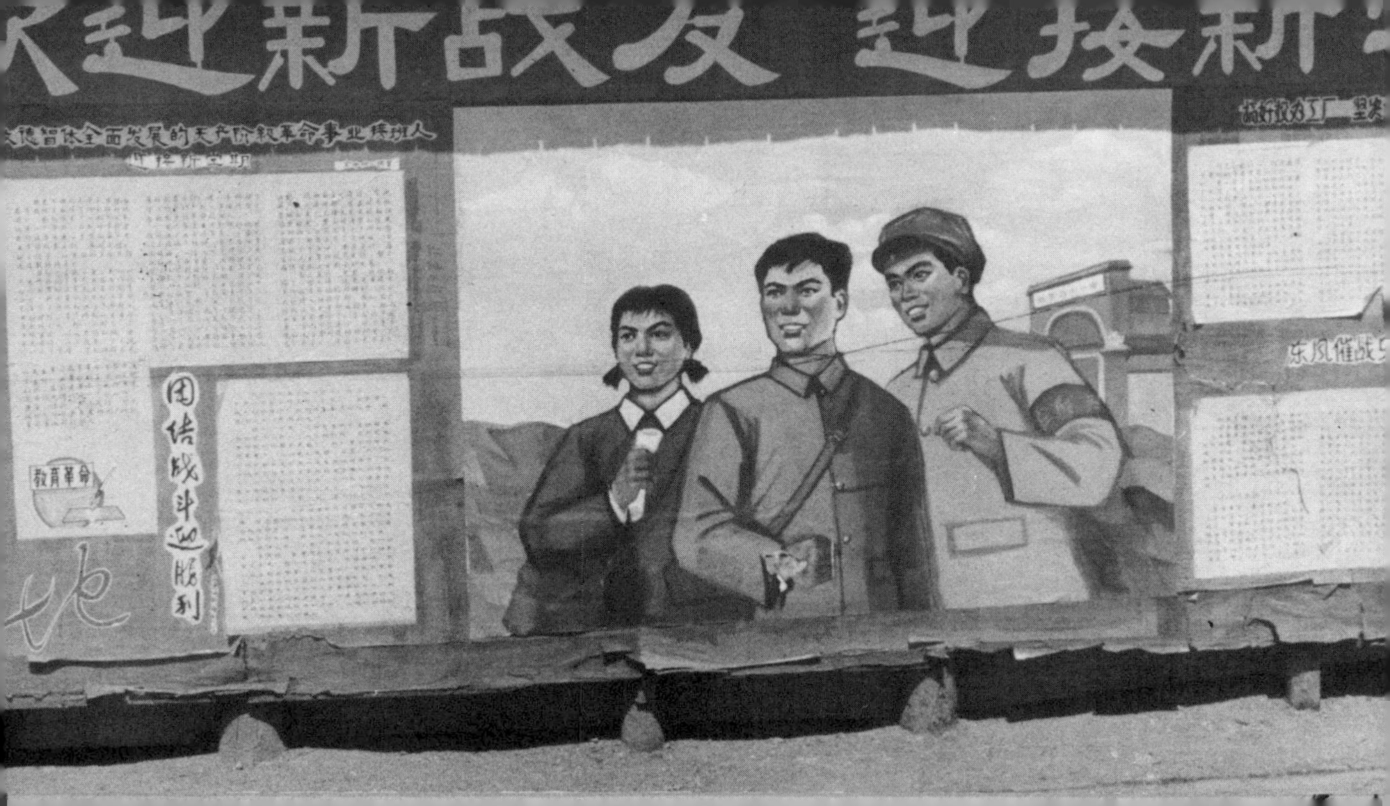
迎新战友 迎接新
德智体全面发展的无产阶级革命事业接班人
团结战斗迎胜利
教育革命
东风催战

型号 MQ8200
编号 94
体积 4.73×2.20×2.00米
毛重 7000公斤

$\left(\dfrac{2}{3}x + \dfrac{3}{4}y\right)^2 \qquad (4x+5y)^2$

$\dfrac{4}{9}x^2 + xy + \dfrac{9}{16}y^2 \qquad (2)$

(1) $4x^2 + 14x + 49$

$= (\sqrt{7m})^2$

(3) $x^2 + 12x + 121$ (4)

x^6

$4a^2 b^2 \div$

复习字词

磨亮　镰刀　寻找　挖草药

学农　园地　东西　史向东

图上　谈谈　返过　人粪尿

肥料　圈肥　叶子　　草木灰

鸡粪　羊粪　菠菜　　提问题

茄子　南瓜　黄瓜　　这件事

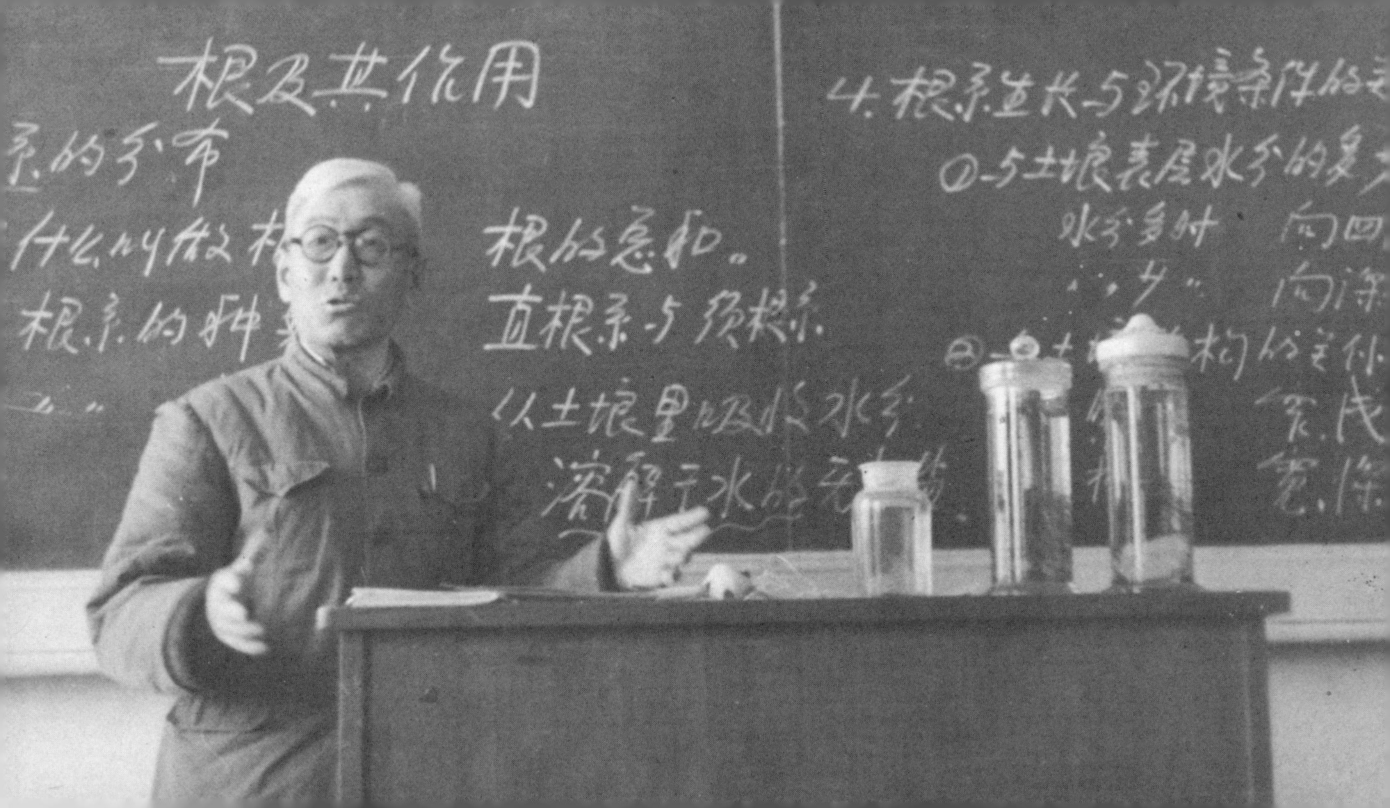
根及其作用
直根系与须根系
4. 根系生长与环境条件的关系
①与土壤表层水分的多少
从土壤里吸收水分

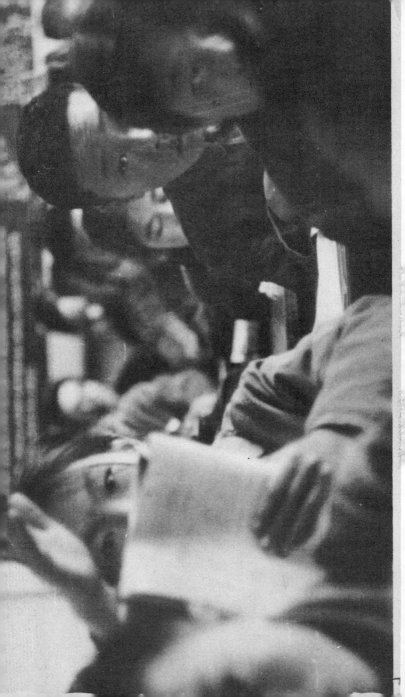

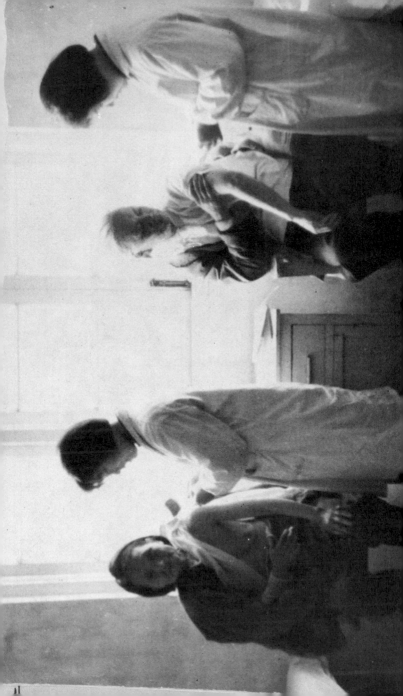

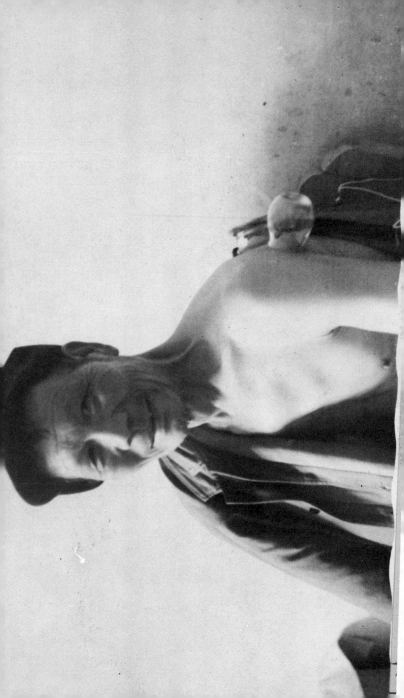

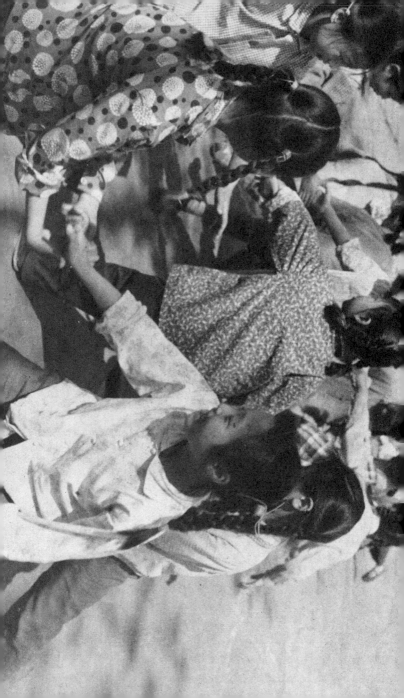

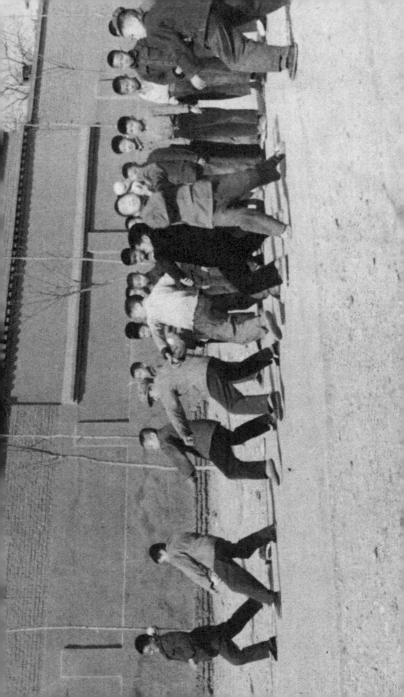

Torn and peeling red fists, sleeves drawn to the ragged elbows, clench and batter the grey Sian city-walls; light rain cooling it, cools the big-character posing, stripped-tough and rippling muscle papering over the shabby-clean mud-cake and grey-wall housing, red flags flying and topping-out the pinnacles of scaffolding-poles on grey flat-blocks, blockish as bunkers of five storeys.

Chimney factory-smoke springs from the wet ground.

Carts loaded with coke, bicycles-on-coke-loaded-on-carts, pass the city-wall.

Blue-grey columns cycle by, on gleaming black frames, grey tyres rubbering the wet roads.

A few broken windows, cut-glass, let in jagged, jet-black, black-mirror reflections (from an unfavourable angle), of moving watery clouds, plate-black negatives on an X-Ray sky.

'We are still poor , we have oxen instead of
machines. We must carry with poles, across
our shoulders.'

Roofs are thatch;

        mud;
        tile;
        bricks on tarpaulins;

huts, houses, sheds, shed-houses, animals running, children
waving, are set back by hummocks and hillocks, brick-heaps
and fences, from the roadside.

> 'But, no longer are there palaces, pagodas,
> and pavillions, reserved for nobles and
> princes, but everywhere now, the labour-
> ing masses go';

(that is, red doors, inlaid with beaten-brass convolutions of
ormolu dragons; or, dais-and-footstools; or, the dripping of
water-clocks, in some mandarin business.)

Along a spring-pooled and puddled road, comes a little
running, limping, boy ; pushes along a metal hoop, with metal
rod, spinning it on, lets it run away for his waving, and darting on again, hoop circling to a standstill, hoops on, and is
gone, limping.

A small girl, plaits flying, throws a ball to another over
the swaggering, sauntering, crowded pavement, missing a
catch, catching a passer-by on the shoulder, raising their hands
to anxious mouths (sky grey-white with smoke rising, street
freshening pink with spring-blossom); and safe, bend double
in laughter.

48

Big city sounds.

'The rich could bribe the official, the poor could not.'

Heavy baggage lugged to this point; again heaping-up, un-
sifted, in the head; hands rubbed red now, by the blistering
load's weight, sombre waiting, looking into faces.

'My family had only 3 mu of land; one thousand catties of
grain only. Because of poverty, I could not go to the middle
school.'

Listening to coughing, and voices.

'...when Chiang Kai-Shek's generals attacked the Red Army
in Northern Shensi.'

City centre of Shensi province, held smoke, locomotive hooters, ready for sighing a cloud of steam into heavy air.

'I met Chairman Mao during our marching, but unfortunately
I did not have the opportunity to talk to him, and he did not
say anything to me.'

And dark leaves, cool not choking, budding, near to the centre,
veterans of Yenan come to the city, talking, old soldiers telling stories.

'They led me across at night, when the KMT were careless,
when the border was not properly guarded.'

Story-telling, passing out of the light, short of breath, winded,
a grey cylinder of cigarette ash bent long, and beyond its time
for falling.

'With the education of the Party, I gained some knowledge. Education is by remoulding, not force; by raising your consciousness.'

Only a gaunt mountain range's dusty distance, to the North, from the caves of Yenan, rim of Mongolia, the Gobi.

'Wheat, cotton, maize, millet, Wei-Ho river, Sian city, 1.8 million', dark gathering of the capital of a province.

'Moslem people here are called Hui.'

Soldiers, chimneys, posters, barracks, smoke, hooters, carts, children, stirring into movement.

'I recalled', coughing, 'my past sufferings, and was moved to tears at the moment of liberation.'

A barrack's early morning bugle, in stiflings of provincial silence; a city waking to locomotives, and, perhaps, far-away music; early voices, through the trees, of children running on a cinder-track, watery rays of smoky sun resting on the sky-line of chimneys and pagoda-roofs ;red flags unstirring.

'I am one of the intellectuals myself. At one time, I was one of the editors of the Liberation Daily. I received a bourgeois education.'

Steam-trains shunting into a coupling chain-reaction.

110

'I was born ninety kilometres from Mao Tse-Tung's birth-place. I was not aware that Liu Shao-Chi's line was obstructing our work, because my political consciousness was not developed.'

Waggons clash up the line into the misty faintness; distant music starts up into the dull cool dawn, on loudspeakers.

'I was a primary school teacher. I went to Shanghai to borrow money for the journey. Underground comrades made contacts for me, and thus I came to Sian, last station before the liberated area.'

Women dipping brushes, barely stirring, painting the lines white, on ash-grey grey-black running-track cinder, and shovelling white powder-lime with the tips of spades, edge it, tipping it on tip-toe into paint-buckets, buds crinkling into full unfurled green leaf; ash at last falling from a fag-end.

'I came down to Sian from the North, after its liberation.'

A man alone, kneeling on gravel, weeding a flower-bed, stocking the green weeds in a pile, beside the thin privet hedges and the sparrows; a man and his daughter, squatting at the road's edge, talking.

49

'Big in the belly and small at the mouth,
     put it in the well, and watch it tilt over.'

This is a hard birth, (no real water), pangs of dry effort in a tribal period, and a light-voiced museum-midwife, lips pursing, speaking drily, hips thrust forward in a short jacket, shows the prehistoric vessel.

> 'Investigation may be likened to the
> long months of pregnancy, and solving a
> problem, to the day of birth.'
> (*Oppose Book Worship*, May 1930)

'From necessity, these bowls were made. The shape of jars and gourds was based on actual necessity, and practice; narrow spouts for a thin stream of water, a large lip for a broad pouring. They knew this from practice', flint-minded, speaking lightly.

> 'Whoever wants to know a thing has no
> way of doing so, except by coming into
> contact with it.'
> (*On Practice*, July 1937)

Through the covered excavation's hangar-window, you may see grass, and fields, heavy carts pulled into mud-courtyards, stockades for pigs, and chickens; here, the dry bones of children (in urns), dead-clay, graves gouged-out under the feet, erections and burials, dry diggings, with sparrows in the girders.

> 'When we look at a thing, we must examine
> its essence, and treat its appearance merely
> as an usher at the threshold, and once we
> cross the threshold, we must grasp the
> essence of the thing; this is the only reli-

112

able and scientific method of analysis.'
(A Single Spark Can Start A Prairie Fire,
January 1930)

Dug-in; concrete, a stone-age. 'We do not give explanations, for the sake of explanation, and not merely of ancient wonders and beauty; but of men who used these stone tools, of their actual practice to create society, and of the real struggle by men, for existence.'

'It is well known that when you do anything, unless you understand its actual circumstances, its nature and its relations to other things, you will not know the laws governing it, or know how to do it, or be able to do it well.'
(Problems of Strategy in China's Revolutionary War, December 1936)

'Thus, by fishing, they found out the shapes of fish, and by this means could paint them, drawing pictures on pottery of the world of nature. When they painted black or red fish on the bases of large bowls, it showed that human beings were mastering nature. Design in art is a reflection of human beings, of the summing-up of experience, and of living people's creation. Present arts should also serve the present.'

'Man has constantly to sum up experience, go on discovering, inventing, creating, and advancing. Ideas of stagnation, pessimism, inertia and complacency, are all wrong.

113

They are wrong because they agree
neither with historical facts of social
development over the past million
years, nor with the historical facts
of nature known to us.'
(*Report on the Work of the Government,
to the First Session of the Third National
People's Congress of The People's
Republic of China,* December 1964)

'The animals had to struggle against nature, if they wanted
to continue living'; (no easy passage through the stony past,
scratching the arid surface in silence). Round-shouldered, the
guide smiles faintly, her hair wired with a metal head-band,
feet on clay and sand, grey-yellow; speaking softly on com-
pacted hard ground.

She says,

> "We used the flint axe-stones, to see if
> it was possible to cut down trees with
> them. To cut down a sapling three
> centimetres thick, took six minutes",

shifting her position beside iron pillars.

> "Yet, it is not tools, but man who
> is the decisive factor in combating
> nature."

Here are holes for stockade-posts, cellars dug-out for neo-
lithic grain-stores;

grit, rock, clay, stone, sand;

114

the ground split open below the surface, and dry as dust;

a stony staring at the dead centre, in roofed-over silence;

a dry river-bed, a river-bank, under girders, and sparrows darting down to the bed-rock.

> 'People were frightened by lightning; they
> imagined gods. That is how they were op-
> pressed. When their houses fell, they crush-
> ed the clay, and built again. In the end, the
> houses became ruins, and covered with dust,
> people moving elsewhere.'

Beyond the window, is a red billboard: 'THE DEVELOP-
MENT FROM THE KINGDOM OF NECESSITY TO THE
KINGDOM OF FREEDOM CAN NEVER STOP!'; and over
a stone-bridge, treading the highway, the passage of carts and
crowds; life-lines.

50

Stand in the entrance of a brown country-pagoda (T'ang);
see the broad magnolia, spreading its branches: fingers-and-
hands in fists of blossom.

(On the flagged, squared, terrace, are spread circles of
children under the branching trees. They are clapping their
hands, and calling, in big games of darting around the circle.
There is a circling illumination of faces, chasing, grabbing, and
a clasping of hands.)

Listen to the tramping-up, and clumping feet climbing the (thumping) wooden steps of the pagoda-tower;

look down the yawning, red-pillared, stair-well;

touch the black-marble tablets, blocks of black scriptures set in the walls;

climb to the first balcony, balustrade, and coping.

Now, you can see the clay village-wall, mud-plastered, bulging; a lych-gate, with a barred window; hear the shouts of children below, feet thudding; peach-pink blossom-branches at the nostril, near roofs in a clutter of tiling, and thrown stones; sheds, hens-through-foliage, courtyard-clusters of walls, roofs and branches; trees greening, at the elbow.

Climb higher;

rising above the entrance-gateways, look down into courtyards, over the grey roofs, and the thatch laid on tiles;

now see the washing, hanging, and a woman sitting (leaning) against a mud-wall in her courtyard, sewing, heaps of straw flecking the beaten-bare courtyard ground, chickens pecking at her feet;

higher, a stagnant green pond, wicker-baskets, and a black pig walking through a courtyard-gateway, and down its stone-stairs, his tail perhaps curling;

rising, a toy horse is rolling in hay, a girl in a courtyard sorting objects (or vegetables), little white-enamel bowls around her, and small cows sitting dark on dust;

see the hen, (your eye narrowing to a neck darting and re-tracting) walking before a girl sitting on a stone, eating from a bowl with quick (invisible) chopsticks; and finishing, going soundless indoors, or disappearing;

and rising, smaller; coming out with, perhaps, a bowl, and passing, say, heaped firewood, and a miniature grey-wooden handcart, long-shafted, she sits down to eat again, lost for a moment and found, dwarfed in a corner.

At the highest recession, sheer, a mere platform and hand-rail in the air, bird's eye telescoped and reeling downwards, human and animal figures are moving in minimized squares and rectangles, appearing and disappearing, dotted and track-ed along lines and in scarrings. This is only a small, walled, en-circled village, the sun shining quiet. The minute hay-clumps, tiny ground-spots and scrapings, the microscopic confetti of white hens on beige flatness, pink-sprinkled, the mapped earth green-striped and yellow-striped to the pale sky-line, (dust in suspension), are near-nothings.

Down again; head couched down, cheek pressed resting on his hand's back, nose to the wrist-bone, arms bent and crumpled under his face, knotted fingers spread under and over his temple, legs in a tangle, white-bearded and dozing, large gnarled stick on the ground, there is an old man, lying on his side, full-length in the sun.

A goliath.

51

Metal buckets, crushed male faces and voices nodding and listening; currents of spa steam-heat, (in the magnolia court-yard of the Five-Door Pavillion), flowing fast, under stone

covers; and purple-cheeked, cool plump smiles, caps, blue
lapels, and Mao-badges..

> "This is the bed; here Chiang Kai-Shek
> was sleeping!"

There is a pressing, blue-jacketed, admiration of the position, in concrete, in the dry light room.

Through the open doorway, are water and limpid willows,
blossom and a faint breeze.

A white bedspread.

A shot (in 1936) fired in the night.

Nodding and savouring, (earnest, or eager), the guide says:

> "His troops were in big rebellion",

soldiers creeping up on him, sleeping at his spa, a close con-
spiracy of gleaming, sun-burned, full-pink faces, agog now to
hear him, taken, guarded, back to Sian, once upon a time.

Breaths are held, blue caps not moving, clustered peasants
and soldiers, more pressing.

> "He clambered out of this window";

and,

"You see here the bullet-hole, here the
broken window."

In the strangenesses of concrete and chlorine, the fresh
dry smiling fills all faces, vertically confined, packed in a
small room.

"In his sleeping garments",

gold gleaming, and eyes twinkling, in immobilized ruddy
merriment,

"And one shoe only",

laughter pent, caught up too pressing, and,

"He had taken off his false teeth",

an outbursting of arms clutching, speaking-on over burst
laughter and relish, and,

"He left in such a hurry through this
window here, foot on the ledge so",

guffawing,

"Out into the gardens",

(out into the air's balm, and there, girls are passing, twirling
sprigs of spring-blossom in their fingers, strolling by the pool-
side, and the darting fishes); and,

"He forgot to put in his false teeth, so he
ran away without teeth",

laughter punching the blown-up ballooned air, and in explosions breaking the room down;

> "One shoe, one shirt, and it was cold
> winter",

the walls shaking and falling, Chiang Kai-Shek bursting out
of confinement, and, in moonlit terror, running past the ancient lakes and green-tiled, upturning pavillions, and up the
strange hillside.

Up terraced grey steps he went (you go), leaping over the
wall, red-lacquered gates barred and bolted, through willow
groves, small conifers, and green bamboo; (you) padding up
the pink, sandy, blossoming hillside, and under a sudden
slogan ('WORKERS OF THE WORLD UNITE!'), strung blazing over the shrubs in flower, (he) running at sheer cliff-hills,
riven and gouged, gorged, chased by laughter; running, cloven-
footed, against the current, dry-mounted, pumping up the
hillside paths through trees, to find a cave to hide in;

(he) fooled, caught in a cleft-stick, (you) hot-breathing, desperate in warm sun and out of condition, heart bursting in
an uphill struggle, (he) foot-falling in the cold night air, ridiculous and terror-struck in pyjamas, limping, shinning-up at
a cleft in the rock-face, scraping and skin-barked in toe-holds,
perching, dried-up, sunk in a hole, toothless, ridged vertical,
holed-up;

(he, you) looking-down, dizzied, at the ancient, dragon-
curling, Pavillion of High Morale,

> "The workers and peasants gave it a
> new name after liberation,"

laughing,

> "The Catching Chiang Kai-Shek Pavillion",

120

at fields of blossom-trees, and sandy pathways, oasis hot-
springs of pools, and pavillions;

(you, he) looking up at a sandstone pinnacle, generalissimo
caught at the summit, heart beating and pumping, hot, blocked and breathless, gulping in the freshest spring fragrance of
blossom and green willows, held-up and staggered, by the
whole situation.

52

A girl's laughter, dying quiet; and you are sinking in warm
spa-water, streaming into liquefaction, bodiless, and slowly
floating-up, buoyant, time out of mind, weightless, light-
headed;

('It became famous two-thousand, eight-
hundred years ago, in the Western Chou
dynasty; only the Emperors, the nobility,
and the KMT reactionaries used it');

steam rising, engulfed alone and dozing, lying in a hot-spring,
dreaming, self idling in oblivion, and curling, foetal, in steam;
floating up to the bath-house ceiling, disappearing through
the open skylight, and into the courtyard; swirling over the
corner gables, the red-and-green lacquered beam-ends of the
bath-house; the sound only of the tap, here, dripping; listening, unstirring.

Your dusty tired clothes, mess of life, lie on the dead deck-
chair, old grey wood, faded grey canvas.

A creaking door slams, in the cold-concrete corridors.

It startles all softness into arousal, standing still.

Hard cold water lashes the body, glistening, to its senses.

Outside, (cheeks warm and purpled, tips of ears tingling, wet-hair plastered and clinging), a faint breeze stirs the deep idyll-green lake; an heraldic stone-pavillion, an hallucination, stone-still, stands on the water in exhilaration, (as if floating, body bursting); late-afternoon sun shines on strolling crowds, soldiers and old peasants taking the waters; blown hot and cold, still floating and alone; their green-and-blue reflections spreading a revolution, circling into deep water, sitting on stone-balustrades at the lake-side.

'This is the time of the spring outing for many people. Some have journeyed from their communes two-hundred-and-forty li, liking to take baths here during Peach-Blossom Time. It is called Peach-Blossom Water, and people think it better for their health, at this season.'

You stare in arousal at dark-pink floral and geometrical tiled floors, tables cigarette-and-match laid; at potted palms, swollen shrubs, and flowering-plants pulsing on carved wooden stands, in a contained and ancient pavillion, perfumed; at wavering smoke, pulling and curling to the high, painted, ceiling; at the sunlit cliff-side, and the grey-pink hill-houses, evanescent and contracting in the purple doorways, (the pavillion pillars, Mao-crowned);

a dark, blood-pumped, red, fluctuating in the mind's palpitation.

53

Out in the open country;

wheat-fields in sunlight, cliff-like sandy hills, tunnelled and
basking, or shadowed chasms, deepening; the hundreds in the
fields, oxen-teams ploughing sunwards, a boy leading a white
goat somewhere; over the Wei-Ho river, low water, lost in ex-
panses of sand;

a dog running widly in the rays, between the furrows of spring-
green wheat, still sun-lit;

quiet lines of girls, hoeing in the strips of wheat, sand sunny,
preparing for cotton;

children, standing in sunbeams, and crouching, weeding with
baskets, small bodies in sunshafts;

red flags caught in a breeze, leading the men in from work,
walking slowly along dusty roads, returning for the day to
the village;

      into the village, the sun setting, carts
      returning;

      women and men, roped (or strapped) across
      the shoulders, tugging handcarts;

      columns of handcarts, turning grey out-of-
      sunlight, carrying huge loads of long-
      planking, heaved and dragged forward;

      a big man running, in a last flaring,
      into the clustered, tumbled village,
      within the shafts of his cart, two ponies

in front of him, one behind, all trotting
together;

two sheep sleeping, on a high-loaded hay-
wain, sun rosy-amber at the horizon.

The caves, in the jutting cliff-outcrops, are abandoned by
light, sinking and sombre. The trees are pink-leaved, in a sun-
spot.

In the village, the day is dying; sandstone-grey, and caught
by a last ray: pink-mud houses. Great brown oxen and buffalo,
horns whirling, walk the street home, heavy-going. One is
tethered to a bicycle, wheeling along slowly, men sleeping
through the village on carts, a creaking slow-motion under
the first star, into dusk. Two children, with red ribbons and
padded clothes, stand in a jumble, sunless, on stacked grey-
concrete pipes, touching a wall newspaper, as if reading.

An orange cat stands in its own light, on the rim of a stone
mortar, while a boy mixes and pounds a white paste with a
pestle. A dim pig, tethered to a tree, is fading; women are
sweeping up grey clouds of dust, with their longhandled
brushwood-brooms, in closing courtyards; a man on a roof
turning to silhouette, in the set sun.

Old carts by the roadside are hopeless in this light.

The small trestle-tables were laid for those who passed this
way on foot, or by cart, or bicycle. Their rows of tea-glasses,
(for a coin), are tepid and diluted by twilight; undrunk, dark-
tinted, and still tended by an old black-padded woman, far
passed into silence.

A man dyed grey, resting, leans back on his back-pack at the road's edge; and a tiny girl, whose cheeks might be florid, ruby, or the colour of a rosy plum in sun, stands darkened, (by the day's last ebbing into night-light), to a black flower, a night-shade.

In the village, under awnings of lean-to sheds, family-groups of peasants are sipping, supping and eating, evening lamps lit. Horses, ponies, asses are standing at troughs, feeding for the night-time. A dark man in a porchway is sleeping in a chair, as the chill sets in, rickety table and cold tea-pot beside him, chickens pecking into the darkness.

An old man stands in the dark, smoking. This is a red pin-point, and a soft nightfall.

54

He is insignificant, perhaps merely some youth (hair, cropp-ed to the scalp, seems to show a young man's shorn skull under bristle), smoking, sitting in an armchair, small blue cap on his head.

But his hands are shaking.

> 'I could not swallow the millet, since I
> was only used to rice.
> I had to learn to eat it; and steamed
> bread also.
> I was not familiar with the North.
> I came from Hunan province.'

Animation starts in his eyes, but his lips are cyanosed by long catchings of breath, nostrils flared, with old efforts.

'I left home one day, nearly thirty
years ago, to join the revolution,
without anyone noticing.'

Hands wasting thin, all finger-joints and knuckles, he has a boy's quiff; a brush of hair starting up, late.

'I was passed from person to person,
sent from one place to another,
travelling Northwards.'

His hands and legs are trembling, a sclerosis, shaken off, holding his legs down.

'I reached the Eighth Route Army's secret
office, here in Sian city. I was led across
country, at night, into the liberated area,
a different world, where men were equal.'

Cigarette ash falls on his lapels, and jacket.

'Since I was a southerner, I was only
used to rice, and could not swallow
the millet.'

Going, he stands at the top of the stairs, high-shouldered with hard breathing, a figure passing out of the light. Illness

can thin and pinch a face hard, into youth. He waves, going
down into the dark.

55

Sit down in a soldiers' brimming night-hall, strange sounding,
resounding; and listen to the plucked strumming, the smoky-
city night-performance, in the barrack-dark music-hall. It is
ugly, drab and foggy with heavy tobacco, thickened with dark-
olive clothing, brown wooden seating, plank flooring, and
smoking (up to the dark ceiling); veils of smoke curling, and
wreathing in whorls, through light-shafts of spotlights, spot-on
the children's singing orange-and-pink faces, and delicate tam-
bourine-dancing.

The smokiness is charcoal-loaded, the smoke of a dark city,
air and aroma of soot-chimneys, old concrete, factory and hut
smoke-stacks, coal-tenders, night-leaves, and darkened blossom,
trees in umbrage, toned-down, awaiting the daylight; bronchial,
with cheap tobacco and troops, (no warlords, no brasshats), unloaded into music and dancing.

Brawn's grave power watches the light, the stage bright to
whiteness. The plucking and strumming, the squeeze-box and
children's dances, bear the brunt of the audience, sombre
bronze-dark hundreds, mobilized and smoking, legs crossed,
muscled arms folded.

Or, elbows-on-thighs, hands-on-cheeks, they lean forward,
facing the music, the gleam of brows and spectacles catching
the stage-light, the children hemmed-in, backed-up by a brig-
ade of soldiers, surrounded, breadth of the hall brown-chaired,

and swallowed-up in smudges of smog-darkness, and a dark
drone of voices.

Air smoke-tasting; cheroots; boys'
drums thudding; brazen trombone and
trumpet; high fluting and stringed
thrumming; braids' skipping and
silken dancing, to a climax;

stormy applause, a thunder hollowed-
out by planking, dark packed crowd
in the smoke, children bowing and
scraping, clapping a broadside, and
rising;

everything drubbing the air in a
reverberation close to roaring, a
gale of hands slapping and pounding
together, rebounding;

pushing-back seats, a crescendo of
voices, clattering and thumping, the
doors opening;

a thousand boots on the flooring,
gruff greetings and fierce hand-
shakes, a cool filtering of leaves
(and spring air) through the dark
doorways;

and, nearer, light voices of
children chattering on the stage,
still high and braced, dolled-up,
in white light for projection, not
yet come down from their drama,
orange faces larger than life, and
gazed at by the last-leavers;

becoming merely kids now, talking,
and laughing together, as the hall
empties.

56

An old man, with a dark stick and string-thin white moust-
aches, walks past a cold magnolia in new bloom, haltingly at
the end of the cobbled pathway, briefly looking round, over-
cast.

On a cold, grey, smoky early morning, (spring factories
smoking), of jade-green tiled roofs and chilled bells ringing,
you are shivering and disjointed.

Flying, jagged, horses gallop their stone sinews to the
strength of a vertical dead-stop; haunches stopped; standing
in a show-case, on ceremony; caught rising, in a museum; a
stone-dead rearing; a funeral vaulting.

Stacked in a deep-black corner of the Sian Bell Tower, on
the stone-paved floor, stiff sky ash-grey, are twenty red flags,
with thick fifteen-foot bamboo poles, put away for a flourish,
for the next fluttering ceremonial, to be set up in triumph
and roaring, red in the open.

Savage gryphons stand, grave-steles in deadly museum air,

    ('He who opens the coffin must die at once'),

beaking fear into the hearts of the poor people;

giant bull-necked oxen, tongue-tied, muscle-in on a dead infanta's gold necklaced burial;

dancing figures, huntsmen, and two-thousand slaves (frozen in slate), sing a Han paean for a rich baby's mausoleum inhumation;

grey iguanodon-jaws, roaring power and funerary terror,

> ('The ruling class wanted to frighten people
> from opening this coffin'),

standing guard, over a noble child's lost interment.

Soldiers are sweeping the streets, with grey brooms the size of small saplings, a brittle rustling across brushed ground; standing, feet cold.

An old woman's half-brick memorial, rough-carved, found on the ground somewhere, is glassed over, in a museum,

> ('My name is Yuan. My mother died'),

some peasant, left on the surface in cold blood; a small urn-burial.

Trees, prepared for transplanting, lie sideways, up-ended along the pavement; earth, clumped around the roots, is held in wicker-matting, string-tied.

57

They are pushing tree-trunk telegraph-poles, twenty-feet

long, balanced on small hand-carts, sacking and clothes covering the pole-ends where they are pushing, because their hands hurt; a child suddenly pushing to help, an infant's hand on the dead-weight, breaking away, and going down a cindery side-street, a black hen gawking.

> 'You see, one rich tomb is of a noble
> girl-child, the other poor stone is of an
> old labouring woman. The price of this
> child's burial and ornament was enough
> for a thousand peasants, such as she,
> to live on for a year long. We may use
> this coffin, to expose such exploitation
> of the labouring people; such crimes of
> the ruling-class against the poor peasants.'

A man is scrubbing clothes on the pavement in an enamel basin.

A cigarette, (socketed in a small bowl), upended, is in a vertical position at the tip of a reed-holder, like a magician's balancing act; a man puffing, moving unevenly, shakily, over hard rough ground, smoking; the cigarette is standing upright.

> 'From the Drum Tower, a drum was beaten
> to tell the people of the city what time it
> was',

evening and morning; men hammering and sawing, before you.

Beside the delicate bamboo trees, carved on black slate; or, the gold, agate, and jade graces, and trophies (portion and proportion of riches, precious scruples in the museum-balance),

131

you make your cold weighing of values; a boy in sawdust,
planing to and fro to a smoothness, leaning forward, touching
wood with his finger-tips.

Tu Fu, the poet, says in a showcase:

> 'The noble family's wine and meats
> Have all gone to waste.
> But on the way, along the road,
> See the bones, and wasted bodies,
> Of the poor people.'

> His successor says, in a blue cap,
> 'The workers came here in the
> cultural revolution to revise the
> explanations, for a critical under-
> standing, not to feel admiration, as
> of old aesthetes for mere beauty,
> but to bring the past to a point.
> They were responsible for the
> suggestion that the brick, in the
> peasant grave, should be put along-
> side the rich coffin of the noble
> child, to be an important lesson.'

Tree-trunks are heaved upright (sun-break, mind firing),
big roots deep-planted. They are tamping the rammed and
thudding earth with sand, burials slammed with spades.

58

Along a back-lane's cluster of houses, and a bumpy side-
walk, you pass one warren-doorway after another (people

peeping); and go into a small deserted inner courtyard, a cubby-hole of flagged stone, a narrow swept covert, silent. There are, here, merely sheltered whitewashed rooms, stone-floored and sparse-furnished; and a lilac-tree's thin blossoming branches, unmoving.

On a wall, is a sepia photograph of men, women and children, standing in a brown desert among moon-mountains, holding their baggage, their dust-blurred faces faded, or tired; and a map of a route, a trail of arrows pointing northwards through the water-colours, over hand-painted crags, pastel-brown tinted but sabre-toothed, ink-jagged.

(In the dust outside, there was a small boy in split trousers, rolling onto his back, cock in the air, tumbling over.)

Tan Ping says,

> "Even the pedlars and rickshaw-drivers
> in the lanes were spies. In rooms above
> the courtyard, were plainclothes men,
> peeping";

a window, sidelong, above the lilac.

> "There were spies in the lanes and
> streets, who sold chickens and
> cigarettes; and spies, who were
> rickshaw-pullers. I was sent here in
> 1938. In this house, the volunteers
> were questioned. In one year, ten-
> thousand revolutionary young people
> made the journey from here, over the
> mountains", (a thick-wristed, short, waving),

"to Northern Shensi, to Yenan and to
the liberated base-areas. Because we
could not accuse the poor labouring
people of this neighbourhood of being
spies, we had to use cunning to test
whether they were spies, or true
labouring people. One supposed rickshaw-puller sat, (waiting and idling
in the lane) for two days, without
custom.

We asked, how could his family live?

A comrade disguised himself as a high-
ranking KMT-officer, came from the
direction of the railway-station, and
said to the rickshaw-puller:
'Take me to the South Gate!'

On the way, he told the poor puller
to run faster and faster, kicking him
hard because he did not run fast
enough, as KMT-officers usually did.

The puller stopped in a side-street,
and said: 'I cannot run faster; I
have not pulled a rickshaw before'.
He showed our comrade, the pretended
high-ranking officer, his pass, saying,
'I am not a real puller. Please get off,
and hire another'.

Our comrade leapt off, and came back
here, and told us that the rickshaw-
puller who was always standing in the
lane was a spy."

He pulls at his cap, and refolds his arms, thrusting them
together into an arm-lock, laughing lightly.

He sits squarely at the table. The room is unfrequented, a matter of dry-flaked whitewash, and uninhabited shadows. He has a broad, bristled face, bland and steady. He sits squarely at the table, a stalwart, arms folded.

'I joined the Fourth Route Army half-
way along its Long March. As a guide
to them, I crossed the Snow Mountains of
my region, and the Grasslands. In the
deep snow, we suffered heavy losses',

both swarthy and youthful, with heavy eyebrows, a dark-blue cap casting a faint shadow at his eyes.

'It took two days to climb the side of
the Wu-Tang mountains. We ended the
first day's climbing on the mountan side,
waiting. We set off again at midnight,
because we wished to cross its peak
before next midday, since, at midday,
there would be a great snow-storm. Some
comrades could not by any means breathe
the air, had nose-bleeding, and the
fainting-sickness, many falling and dying.'

He wears a light-blue jacket and trousers, and a light-blue Mao-badge, watching. He sits squarely at the table; or, looks briefly at a wristwatch with its broad watch-strap; or, sits back, fingers tapping the table-edge.

Outside, in the lane, a young girl (hunched, intent) was wobbling on a bicycle, a man running along past the houses, full-chested, beside her, a pacing and steadying hand at the saddle; and, at its speeding, giving-up and letting-go, but still large striding, gesticulating but quickly outdistanced, and fall-

ing away. He pulled up to a standstill, waiting in the gutter,
uncertain, shading his eyes.

> 'I came from Szechwan. My family was
> poor. I tended cows. I was a cowherd.
> When the Red Army came to my town, I
> was thirteen. The landlords and despots
> ran away. The poor remained. I joined them.'

He is lit up briefly by laughter, refolding his arms, in-
different.

After a silence, the cowherd said,

> "When your Long March begins, I will
> be your guide."

59

Flying, desert-climbing, up stone-barren (rattling) hills,
flapping; and stretching dead-brown, upwards, over bulging
Shensi mountains, dry as the sand-dune moon; flying upwards,
sun on the wing-flaps, straining in space, hovering and wavering, ready to plummet;

ailerons quivering over a plunging grand-canyon, shadow of
a liliput light-plane falling on sand, on Northern guerrilla-
ranges of giant ferns'-spines and dead ridges, serrated edges
and ambushes cut into palm-fronds, felled-flat and gigantic in
fossil-dust, and locked into stone jig-saws;

over grey (a faint road-track far below, running along a roaring ridge-summit) ravines, and furrowed escarpments, wings

tipping and balancing over terraces, groovèd and turning-
around hill-bases, like ribboning sand-ridges at low-tide, like
hard sea-floor sand-bars, to the high brown horizon;

now, banking down (rigid) into a steep nose-drive, dropping
like a stone into a narrow valley, you come plumb down the
vibrating centre, taxi-ing among towering and lowering cliff-
sides, peopled and beehived with cave-holes.

There are figures (some drowning, in the wheels' dust-
storm and feathering) working the sand, at a stone's throw.

Distant quarry-blasting rattles the airport windows, quivering the concrete.

"Here, there were thirteen-hundred years of history, from the
Sui dynasty until Chairman Mao entered Yenan, on July 1st,
1937. Here, he stayed thirteen years. Here, were carried out
important revolutionary and practical activities. Here, he
wrote important theoretical works. Volume Four of his
Collected Writings contains 158 articles, of which 122 were
written in Yenan, including 'On Contradiction', and 'On
Practice'."

> 'In the process of practice, a man at
> first sees only the phenomenal side ,
> the separate aspects, the external
> relations of things. For instance,
> some people from outside come to
> Yenan on a tour of observation. In
> the first day or two, they see its
> topography, streets, and houses;
> they meet many people, attend banquets,
> evening-parties and mass-meetings, all

these being the phenomena, the separate
aspects, and the external relations of
things. This is called the perceptual
stage of cognition, namely, the stage
of sense-perceptions and impressions.'
(On Practice, July 1939)

A woman searches in a child's hair, squatting by the roadway, amid stacks of coal.

'That is, these particular things in
Yenan act on the sense-organs of the
members of the observation-group,
evoke sense-perceptions, and give
rise in their brains to many impressions, together with a rough sketch
of the external relations among
the impressions: this is the first
stage of cognition. At this stage,
man cannot as yet form concepts,
which are deeper, nor draw logical ·
conclusions.'
(On Practice, July 1937)

The children are waving, in air thick with dust. The sun is
in suspension. You see the stacked tree-trunks and brushwood,
hovels, and factory-chimneys; the faded and smudged red-
flags, tattered with fluttering and buffeting, stirring limp in
coal-grit, over a factory-entrance.

"Here he set up a number of schools, a Central Party School,
a Marxist-Leninist College, the Political and Military University of Anti-Japanese Aggression, and the Yenan University
and Medical Institute."

138

There is a crack of rock-blasting, a thunder of explosives, drumming panes...

"Here Chairman Mao presided over the Yenan Forum on Literature and Art; and here met Norman Bethune."

> 'We must all learn the spirit of absolute
> selflessness from him, a foreigner, who
> selflessly adopted the cause of the
> Chinese people's liberation as his own.
> A man's ability may be great or small,
> but if he has this spirit, he is already
> noble-minded and pure, a man of moral
> integrity, and above vulgar interests, a
> man who is of value to the people.'
> (*In Memory of Norman Bethune*, 1939)

Rolling echoes, stifled bumping in darkening sand-hills.

"This is the sacred place of the revolution, the end of the Long March"; and

"The people had their hopes in the Yenan caves."

There is a dull thunder, but no rainfall; only a shower of stones somewhere, two tiny children hovering and wavering over a deep-shadowed road-trench, and a cock ruffling its feathers in a heap of rubble.

60

Thin factory-chimneys are smoking black, over the Yenho River, over the Yenan pagoda, over the sepia rockfaces of sandstone, poxed and riven, landmarked with cave-holes, burrowed with eye-openings and tunnelled with dug-outs, eaten away, or fallen.

Here are foodsmells, bed-rolls, towelled-turban head-cloths, chimneys.

You may walk into silent scrub-and-sand courtyards, ledged and walled with long outcrops and standing back-drops of sand-stone banking; cliff-shelves, jutting into the town.

A blue work-jacket hangs on a line, strung between a small tree and a wooden post, a shrub planted in sand.

You pass dug-in honeycomb-warrens of caverns, and shack housing; or stone-built outbuildings, flush against the ledge-face, cave-rooms gone to earth, and hollowed into the cliff-edge sandbanks.

There are lines of washing, patched and faded; children playing.

There are timber-framed and latticed openings for doors and windows, papered over and stuck with green, red, and blue animal-and-flower cut-outs; roofed awnings at the lintels.

There are clusters of jars, wooden buckets, brooms, tools and whet-stones, crowded at the doorsteps.

There are cavernous burrows, and fox-holes, for storage; dark dens of stacked coke, and sleeper-sized timbers, of old iron or brushwood, and masonry-chunks of large-hewn, gleaming, coal-blocks; there are tunnel-curved walls, cut (shelving underground) into the abandoned interior, caving-in; roof falls, tumbled, boarded-up with grey planking, stop-gaps.

There are singing soldiers in the cluttered street, marching.

61

Detonation, and a depth-charge.

Here clenched hands are purple in the cold cave-room; she is tapping her foot on the ground, a little. The curved, tunnelled, roof is plastered and whitewashed; with a grey-brick floor, wooden lattice-work door and window, grey-papered.

"This is Chairman Mao's first Yenan cave-house. Outside, on the terrace, is the place of the first-giving of 'Combat Liberalism', in a speech to the cadres."

There is knocking and blasting in the dropped and jarring hills, a thundered rockfall roaring down the Fenghuang hillside, rolling to a soft footfall on padded ground.

'To let things slide for the sake of peace

and friendship when a person has clearly
gone wrong, and refrain from principled
argument because he is an old acquaintance,
a fellow townsman, a schoolmate, a close
friend, a loved one, an old colleague or
old subordinate, is one type of liberalism.
Or, instead of going into things thoroughly,
so as to keep on good terms, merely
touching on a matter lightly.'
(*Combat Liberalism*, September 7, 1937)

The terracing is in its first green and blossom, the sun
blocked and steeped in dust; you are heavy-headed, standing
still. A photograph of a young man shows him, hands-on-hips,
standing outside the cave-house, on this terrace.

The young girl says,

(giggling) "People live in caves in this area, because it is warm-
er in winter, and cold in summer",

and, with a light lilted inflexion, eyes darting as she speaks,
says,

"This was Chairman Mao's reception-room, this was Chairman
Mao's office",

something in a girl's smiling deep-burrowed, or buried.

'A second type is to say nothing to
people to their faces, but to gossip
behind their backs, or to say nothing
at a meeting but to gossip afterwards.
To show no regard at all for the

principles of collective life, but to
follow one's own inclination. A
third, is to let things drift if they
do not affect one personally; to say
as little as possible while knowing
perfectly well what is wrong...'
(Combat Liberalism, September 7, 1937)

There is a photograph of a young man, working at his desk. A cluster of people is peering and whispering at the doorway behind you. In a glass-case, are the remains of worn quilting.

"Here is the wooden chair where Chairman Mao sat, when he wrote 'On Practice', 'On Contradiction', 'On Protracted War', and 'Combat Liberalism'."

On a raised platform at the cave-end, is a bed.

"He worked day and night in his writing, and became ill. He worked so hard, Chairman Mao did not even notice his canvas shoes being burned by the stove,"

her buff trousers just touching the worn wooden chair-seat, her feet planted before you.

'To be aware of one's own mistakes, and
yet make no attempt to correct them,
taking a liberal attitude toward oneself;
not to obey orders but to give pride of
place to one's own opinions; to hear
incorrect views, without rebutting them,
and even to hear counter-revolutionary

143

remarks without reporting them, but
instead to take them calmly, as if
nothing had happened. These are other
types...'
(*Combat Liberalism,* September 7, 1937)

Two dented metal-boxes, for keeping papers on the Long
March, and turned to writing-tables when the army halted,
(ikons in the half-dark) are set on bare cave-ground. Through
a tear in the paper-window, are faces, and the pulse of low-
whispering voices.

'To see someone harming the interests of the
masses, and yet not feel indignant, nor dissuade
nor stop him, nor reason with him, but to allow
him to continue, forgetting that one is a
Communist; to work half-heartedly, without a
definite plan or direction; to work perfunctorily,
or muddle along — "So long as one remains a
monk, one goes on tolling the bell". These are
other types...'
(*Combat Liberalism,* September 7, 1937)

The air is filled with dust, coal and coke-air. Between blasts,
voices carry down from the high, stilled, hill-side. A crump of
quarry-thunder explodes in a deep chamber; a girl's grey-blue
jacket sleeve, unmoving at the table.

'People who are liberals look upon the
principles of Marxism as abstract dogma.
They approve of Marxism, but are not
prepared to practise it ... these people have
their Marxism, but they have their liberalism
as well — they talk Marxism, but practice

144

liberalism to themselves. They keep both
kinds of goods in stock, and find a use for
each. This is how the minds of certain
people work.'
(*Combat Liberalism*, September 7, 1937)

Shabby sandstone hills, dusty sunshine, tiny figures; cave-
men, perched and working; a girl's fists in her trouser-pockets.

62

'Every comrade must understand that as
long as we rely on the people, believe in the
inexhaustible creative power of the masses,
we can surmount any difficulty, and no enemy
can crush us, while we can crush any enemy.'
(*On Coalition Government*, April 24, 1945)

A cock crowing.

'We should be modest and prudent, guard
against arrogance and rashness, and serve
the Chinese people heart and soul.'
(*China's Two Possible Destinies*, April 23, 1945)

Caked-mud walls, around the small building.

'There is an ancient Chinese fable, called
"The Foolish Old Man Who Removed The
Mountains". It tells of an old man who lived

145

in Northern China long, long ago, and was
known as the Foolish Old Man of the North
Mountain. His house faced south, and beyond
his doorway stood the two great peaks, Taihang
and Wangwu, obstructing the way. With great
determination, he led his sons in digging up
these mountains, hoe in hand. Another grey-
beard, known as the Wise Old Man, saw them
and said derisively, "How silly of you to do
this! It is quite impossible for you few to dig
up these huge mountains". The Foolish Old
Man replied, "When I die, my sons will carry
on; when they die, there will be my grandsons,
and then their sons and grandsons, and so on,
to infinity. High as they are, the mountains
cannot grow any higher, and with every bit
we dig, they will be much lower. Why can't
we clear them away?" Having refuted the
Wise Old Man's wrong view, he went on digging every day, unshaken in his conviction.
God was moved by this and he sent down two
angels, who carried the mountain away on their
backs. Our God is none other than the masses
of the Chinese people. If they stand up and
dig together with us, why can't the mountains
be cleared away?'
(*The Foolish Old Man Who Removed The
Mountains*, June 11, 1945)

Misted stony hills.

'The Communist Party of China has brought
a new style of work to the Chinese people,
integrating theory with practice, forging
close links with the masses, and practising
self-criticism.'
(*On Coalition Government*, April 24, 1945)

Dusty, hard ground.

'We Communists never conceal our political
views. Our maximum programme is to carry
China forward, to socialism and communism,
to this supreme ideal of the future, a future
of incomparable brightness and splendour.'
(*On Coalition Government,* April 24, 1945)

Raked stone floor, slatted wooden benches, paraffin-lamps,
grey-blue walls.

'Without a people's army, the people have
nothing... This army is powerful because all
its members have come together, and they
fight, not for the private interests of a few
individuals, or a narrow clique, but for the
interests of the broad masses, and of the whole
nation.'
(*On Coalition Government,* April 24, 1945)

Grey wooden steps to the platform, portraits on the pro-
scenium, faded-red drawn-up drapes, a long table with a purple
cloth, five wooden chairs facing the empty auditorium, flags,
standards; faded party-banners, hanging.

'The people, and the people alone, are the
motive force in the making of world history.'
(*On Coalition Government,* April 24, 1945)

Damp-marks on the upper wall, running down the white-wash from the upper windows.

> 'Our congress should teach every comrade
> to love the people, and listen attentively to
> the voice of the masses; to identify himself
> with the masses wherever he goes, and, instead
> of standing above them, to immerse himself
> among them; to awaken them; and to set
> going all essential struggles.'
> (*On Coalition Government*, April 24, 1945)

Here is Yangchialing village, "Grand Hall of the Party Central Committee, site of the Seventh National Congress of the Communist Party of China, April to June 1945, where were read 'China's Two Possible Destinies', 'The Foolish Old Man Who Removed The Mountains', and 'On Coalition Government'".

> 'Self-criticism is a hallmark, distinguishing our
> Party from all other political parties. As we say,
> dust will accumulate if a room is not cleaned
> regularly; our faces will get dirty, if they are
> not washed regularly. The proverb "Running
> water is never stale, and a door-hinge is never
> worm-eaten", means that constant motion
> prevents inroads of germs, and other organisms.'
> (*On Coalition Government*, April 24, 1945)

There are white slogan-letters, prized, warped; lifting off the red wooden hoarding by the sandy, swept, pathway; and a soft sound of dry treading, on iron ground.

148

'This army has an indomitable spirit, and is
determined to vanquish all enemies. So long
as a single man remains, he will fight on...
Thousands upon thousands of martyrs have
heroically laid down their lives, for the
people; let us hold their banner high, and
march ahead, along the path crimson with
their blood!'
(*On Coalition Government*, April 24, 1945)

Thin sunlight, dust-laden.

63

You stand, listening to smothered voices from the path,
soft and stifled. In this cave, is a grey-hessian deck-chair, its
(your) feet in fine cave-dust, a bed with a buff awning, and
a small timber table.

'Many writers and artists lead empty lives.'

There is grey muslin for a window, and a filtered view for
the eye, pupil narrowing at a peep-hole.

'You must make up your mind to undergo
a long, and even painful, process of tempering',

and

'It takes a long period of time, at least
eight or ten years to solve it thoroughly.'

Outside, shoes are scuffled, dull suffocated movements.

> 'Since many writers and artists stand aloof
> from the masses, and lead empty lives,
> naturally they are unfamiliar with the
> language of the people.'

> 'The clothes in this story are the clothes
> of the working-people, but the faces are
> those of petty-bourgeois intellectuals.'

> 'Literature and art for whom?'

> 'Take, for instance, the sectarianism in
> literary and art circles.'

> 'There is hardly a writer or artist who
> does not consider his own works beautiful.'

Coming out into the open, breaking the surface (and taking
the air), a girl's voice is gesturing urgently, eyes opening wide.

> 'They do not like the workers' feelings,
> or their manner',

and

> 'At times they are fond of those things,
> too, but that is only when they are
> hunting for novelty.'

At the cave-entrance, there is a mud-walled terrace.

> 'There is no such thing as art for art's sake,
> no art that stands above classes.'

Rooted in fissures, are tiny tares, small as the mind's eye,
minute vetches, purple-blue, in the crevices of the caked-sand
walling.

'The life of the people makes all
literature and art seem pallid by comparison.'

'Otherwise you will have nothing to work
with, and you will be nothing but a phoney
writer, an autocrat, who lords it over "the
lower orders"'.

'The prime need is not "more flowers
on the brocade", but "fuel in snowy
weather."'.

A man in a blue cap, carying a mattock, is standing stock-still
in the path, staring. In the mud-wall, is a roofed doorway to
the dusty pathway up the hillside.

'All art and literature are for the masses
of the people, for their use'.

'Only counter-revolutionary writers
describe the revolutionary masses as
"tyrannical mobs"'.

He is standing quiet, smiling.

'If we had no literature and art, even in
the broadest and most ordinary sense, we
could not carry on the revolutionary
movement and win victory.'

'You will certainly be able to bring
about a transformation in yourselves
and your work, moving your feet over
to the side of the workers, peasants and
soldiers.'

There are grey wiry strands, in a girl's black shiny hair.

'The process may, and certainly will,
involve much pain and friction if you
want the masses to understand you.'

Perching by the fingertips of the topmost branches, ruffling and preening, a crow is keeping its eyes open.

'Your work may be as good as "The Spring
Snow", but if it caters only to the few, and
the masses are still singing "The Song of the
Rustic Poor", you will get nowhere.'
(*Talks at the Yenan Forum on Literature and
Art*, May 2-23, 1942)

The figure with a mattock is moving slowly, in dust-stuffed
air, along an upper-terrace sand-banking.

Up five sandstone steps before you, is a pink, sandstone-
brick, building, small squat place of the Yenan Forum, of
sentences upon literature and art in a seven-windowed room.
There are two small brick-fireplaces, with stone mantels, in
the room's corners, (swept clean), hearths and grates cleared-
out, bare and empty; stools and backless wooden-benches,
around a varnished, battered, dark-brown table.

The crow will have taken off by now, beating it, with a brash black flapping through bare trees, alighting at a safer distance, smoothing its feathers. The man with a mattock is climbing the hillside, dry breathing, going softly.

64

A shepherd's place; a twist of dust under the hill, blurring along the ground, hard-going, dying.

'To come to the revolutionary bases from
the garrets of Shanghai, means not only to
pass from one kind of place to another, but
from one historical epoch to another.'
(*Talks at the Yenan Forum on Literature &
Art*, May 23, 1942)

There is the silence of a fly buzzing in the ear, and a trickle of water on stones. This is merely a scraped patch, surrounded by a dry-stone wall.

"This is the place of the giving of the 'Serve the People' speech".

A clearing, struggling with dust.

There is nothing doing in this dusty light.

Five slogan-characters ('SERVE THE PEOPLE!!') are spaced out on five faded hoardings, set in the hillside.

153

'In times of difficulty we must not
lose sight of our achievements, must
see the bright future, and must pluck
up our courage.'
(*Serve The People*, September 8, 1944)

A scurry, and a cock's crowing; ululation flowering on a
stone, rooting to the ground.

'Wherever there is struggle there is
sacrifice, and death is a common occurr-
ence. But we have the interest of the
people, and the sufferings of the great
majority, at heart, and when we die for
the people, it is a worthy death.'
(*Serve The People*, September 8, 1944)

Stalking the earth, tail-feathers riffling in a blowing wind ;
hot air, goat-bells.

'If we have shortcomings, we are not afraid
to have them pointed out, and criticized.
Anyone, no matter who, may point out
our shortcomings. If he is right, we will
correct them. If what he proposes will
benefit the people, we will act upon it.'
(*Serve The People*, September 8, 1944)

Coming down a defile towards the hill-village, are pack-
horses, pannier-laden, stumbling hooves kicking up dust,
clipping the stone; an old woman, feet hobbled, standing
with a small child.

'All men must die, but death can vary in
its significance. The ancient Chinese
writer, Szuma-Chien said, 'Though death
befalls all men alike, it may be weightier
than Mount Tai, or lighter than a
feather.'
(*Serve The People,* September 8, 1944)

The old woman brushes at the child's face with gnarled
fingers, to prepare him for being seen.

65

'Wherever we go, we must unite with the
people, take root, and blossom among them.'
(*On The Chungking Negotiations,* October 17,
1945)

These were the villages in the base-area of a revolutionary
war; dens and rookeries.

'Here, were held gather-together meetings; here, greeting and
eating together, with the peasants of the village.'

The black flock, light as a feather in dusty light, settles on a
light, green-dusted, tree; croaking, and cawing black; insisting,
as with bare hands.

'What is work? Work is struggle. There
are difficulties and problems for us to

overcome, and solve.'
(On The Chungking Negotiations, October
17, 1945)

'Here the comrades used to carry the water for the peasants,
and clear up their courtyards.'

This is a place of manure, rough dry sacking, oven-ash,
and grey timber; of swept paths, and curved brush-strokes on
the dust; of a broom's wide-sweeping, over stone-hard ground;
of foot-marks.

The swept-out, clay-and-wattle caves cluster in a huddle. Grey
tree-boles are wrapped with frayed straw-ropes.

'Here is the place of military thinking, and leadership; here
the meeting-place of officers of the Liberation Army.'

You may step among the slow sorting of stone, the handling
of grey trestles, and rough-grained hurdles. A column of
women, seen walking a road with spades, is now passing along
these paths, and fading.

'There are no straight roads in the world.
We must be prepared to follow a road
which twists and turns, and not try to
get things on the cheap.
(On The Chungking Negotiations, October
17, 1945)

'From here, they went out to launch armed-struggle; from
here, to negotiate at Chungking with the KMT forces; from
here, they withdrew to save the revolution.'

There is dust on your lips, limp willowy trees weeping, and
drifting. A man, crouching, leans against a wall, head-on-knees,

arms around his head, sleeping. The dry dust pricks the
nostril. A child, in a red jacket (pink-blossom, stepping into
dry light) is making eyes, at the mud-walling.

There is a knot of flowers (in this poor whitewashed
room) covertly smiling, a tremor of children's flower-faces,
pink and bewildering. Girls (arms clasping), are singing for
you, in an empty space, wearing black slippers.

'In this world, things are complicated, and
are decided by many factors. We should
look at problems from different aspects,
not from just one.'
(*On The Chungking Negotiations,* October
17, 1945)

'Here, was the General Headquarters of the Eight Route Army;
here, the place of receiving military reports from field-
commanders; here, was the meeting-place of the Central
Committee; here, was given the report on the Chungking
Negotiations.'

A place of grey timbering, and rough hewings; its rafters plaited, and wattled.

'Hard work is like a load placed before us,
challenging us to shoulder it. Some loads
are light, some heavy. Some people prefer
the light, to the heavy; they pick the light,
and shove the heavy onto others. That is
not a good attitude.'
(*On The Chungking Negotiations,* October
17, 1945)

You may stand in the dust of planking falling, and stunned chisels on stone, of blocks-of-stone carried on poles (trippingly), and balanced along grey gangplanks, of sand dug softly, and spades in gravel. You (idle) listen to the clank of pails pouring water, and the slow stirring. Wet cement is carried quickly, in dripping cloths, running, bulging like knapsacks.

'China's problems are complicated, and our brains must be a little complicated, also.'

A woman, working, breaks off, takes her hair-grip from her hair, re-fixes it, and shoulders her dusty load; lightly placing her foot on the gangplank.

66

Outside, they are going to load a cart with gleanings, the mule waiting, lipping the dust, ears pricking. The old man's thin hands and wrists are lost in such large black sleeves. They say, whispering, "He is an old friend of Chairman Mao', an eye-witness. There is luminescence in his tiny eyes, patched clothes, and thin wasted movements, savouring his reminiscence in uncertain light. He has (wrapped in a red kerchief) old snap-shots of himself when younger, strapping, faded. He plucks at one, long-nailed, fingers slipping and scratching on a black-and-white surface. A man is climbing onto the cart.

They say, "Mao took his hands, and said, 'You are our party's good fighter. We will never forget you'". His long, thin face, bucking up, making merry, wrinkles into a smile, drawn back to the gums. There is a slow hoisting of brush-wood going on, forked and lifted. In the brick-floored, white-washed room, there is an old iron-stove, black stove-pipe running zig-zag, and the end burrowed into the ceiling. The

old man's voice is light with age. He says, "Once, in the days
of Yenan, I heard that Chairman Mao was working in the
fields, not many li from this village. I drove two donkeys
with the wheat of the harvest. I gave it to Chairman Mao."

The man on the cart is heaping and stacking the brushwood. Beyond the mud-wall, there is smoke rising.

They say, outright, in his hearing, "Wang Pu-Ho became
a labour-hero, and led production in this region." He fumbles
the kerchief, absently, picking at the pictures. "Chairman Mao
gave me some hot peppers he had produced on his plot, at
Yangchialing."

The old man's hands are shrunken in his jacket sleeves. Outside, the man on the cart treads in brushwood.

"Then, he said to me, 'Why do you want to
fulfil my labour-task, instead of me?'"

His hands are worked, worn, black-nailed; fingers resting,
clawed, on his thigh. He sits forward.

"I said to him, 'I am a poor peasant.
My mother died when I was eight. We
borrowed money and could not pay our
debts. So we ran away from our native-
land.' I said to him, 'My father and my
small daughter died of starvation. After
you arrived in Northern Shensi province,
we got our liberty,'"

hands stirring;

"'How can we forget your kindness?
Does not Yenan now belong to the people
for ever?'"

He looks round with defiance at such a sentence.

"'So', I said, 'I did your task to ensure
your good health, so that you can fulfil
yours, for the happiness of the other poor
people.'"

They are trampling on the cart, campacting a load, in
silence.

"I journeyed to see Chairman Mao, in
Peking, after the liberation. Why not?
He was my friend, and therefore I
missed him day and night. They said,
'Who is this Wang Pu-Ho?' I got in a
black car, and got to him very quickly",

hands arrowing, point-blank, with quick birdlike movements,
thin twigs limed to catch the moment.

"He asked me to sit next to him at the
table. He said, 'Help yourself. Have nice
steamed bread, and many bowls of food.'
He gave me a new suit of cotton-padded
clothes, because I was wearing my old ones."

A man in the room pushes his blue cap back, and scratches
the boils on his head. The man on the cart is treading knee-deep

in dead wood; the mule restless, and all for going. The old man
stands up spry, bandy with age, hands marked and darkened,
old feet in black-cord sandals. He says,

> "I will not rest on my laurels. I will
> continue to make revolution as long as
> I live",

looking into the faces of those around him. The younger men
laugh like sons; one takes him by the arm.

    They are tying the large load, cut and dried, to the cart,
with ropes.

67

    In a morning pall, birds are chirping (under heavy pressure),
around the deserted museum. The early halls are all echoes
and metal voices, a glass-panelled door slamming, the instruments
of revolution held dead-still in glass-cases, or nailed to the wall.

A man in such a deserted condition may make his own inven-
tory of the apparatus:

> Cap, belt, jacket, trousers, and straw sandals;

> Rifle, revolver, grenade;
> Tin mug, and bowl of millet;

> ('It must not be imagined that, one fine
> morning, all the reactionaries will go down
> on their knees, of their own accord')

> Pointed stick, for plans drawn in sand;

Transparent-thin leaves of the manuscript
of 'Reform our Study', set in red velvet;

('We must not behave like a blind-folded man
catching sparrows, or a blind man groping for
fish, be crude and careless, indulge in verbiage,
or rest content with a smattering of knowledge;
we must rely not on subjective imagination,
not on momentary enthusiasm, not on lifeless
books, but on facts that exist, objectively')

From the window, you see a girl turning to her side, and
spitting on the grey concrete; and the barrack-grey, dry-mud,
loess-hills, which would crumble under a giant's fist, and cascade in a quarry-blasted rolling of clouds, and billows. But
in the room, there is a dead silence.

Item:

Paper, made from grass;

Ink and rollers;

Pens, made from cartridge-cases;

Leaflets;

('TO THE KMT SOLDIERS OF THE NORTH-
EASTERN ARMY: ARE YOU WILLING TO
GIVE UP TWENTY PROVINCES TO JAPAN?
ARE YOU WILLING TO BE SLAVES? NOW
THAT IT IS WINTER, THE LANDLORDS
ARE FORCING RENT OUT OF THE PEASANTS.
YOU MUST HELP YOUR MOTHERS, BROTHERS
AND SISTERS. O, WORKERS, PEASANTS,
SOLDIERS, MERCHANTS, UNITE!!')

A twisted wire holds up a stove-pipe, suspended close below the whitewashed ceiling. There is also a stuffed pony here,
bursting at the seams, (and no charger), once ridden by a com-
mander.

('Rallying millions-upon-millions of people
round the revolutionary government, and
expanding our revolutionary war, we shall
take over the whole of China').

And, beyond the gates, there are soldiers in the road, pushing
carts, earth-laden, creaking and trundling them to town, in a
heavy swaying and rolling.

68

Through the bed of a stream of shallow trickling water, up
a steep path, and shambling through dust, in grey sunlight,
you come to a silent village, (steep fields worked to the sky-
line), still-point of no return;

in a light filtered-down through terraced hillsides, bursting
into blossom, old women (with bound feet) sitting heavily at
their doors, children with dusty faces and uptufted black
hair, wobbling and toppling, noses running, all sound muzzled
by sun, and dust;

a white pig staring, and a hen (at a footfall) fanning its wings,
whirring the air into a quick short-lived flurry.

These are seconds stunned to rest, standing before the mass
of life, the slow saw moving back and forth under the trees
and a foal standing, at the moment of turning to stone, tethered
under an awning, the ox stitting heavily, dozing.

The shepherd, with the slow ambling walk, moves forward
slowly, in padded dusty clothes, his towelled-turban folded
and knotted, baring his blackened teeth; and standing, looks
at the table in the cold cave-room, saying,

> 'I am a shepherd. I looked after the sheep
> of the landlord from the time when I was
> eight-years old. We poor people struggled.
> We made a revolution, and overthrew the
> local despots. We distributed the land to
> the poor and middle peasants. We gave
> plots of land to the landlords also. They
> were forced to change their class nature.
> They had to work it themselves. So their
> paradise can never be restored.'

Along a sandy path, in the peasant-doctor's cavehouse,
are:

> a table;
>
> a deal-cupboard, with shelving;
>
> labelled bottles, and packets;
>
> an abacus;
>
> a mortar-and-pestle;
>
> and small brass scales, for weighing
> in the balance, and meting-out, such
> remedy as is fitting.

Another man in the cave, sitting on a brown wooden-bench
at the table, (and smoking his cigarette to the butt, in pinched
stained fingers), says,

'There were the taxes, which a man
could not count. We had no land to pay
rent, or owings. Four landlords owned
the land of this village. When there was
a famine, friend, we had to sell our sons
and daughters.'

On the table, is a dish of apples, and steam rising from
bowls of tea. The apples are a pastel-yellow, a light rose, and
ruddy: a still-life, in a lair.

He says,

'We have one hundred and seventy-six
households, seven-hundred and eighty-
two people, three-thousand five-hundred
apple trees, one hundred and eighty-six
big animals, thirty-six horses and mules,
one-thousand two-hundred sheep and goats,
and four-hundred and seventy pigs.'

This is the mental-arithmetic of hard labour, and is over-
seen by portraits of leaders on the cave-wall.

Outside, is a small terraced clearing with a heavy stone
table;a stone slab-covered well, and a grey, wooden, plough-
like pump-handle; beyond, a stone-faced tunnel into the hillside, entrance barred and bolted, and covered by a straw-
awning. The old women are at their cave-house doorways,
spinning, or dandling babies, smoke stuffing from soot-blacken-
ed chimneys, in the cliff-wall above them.

The shepherd cuts into an apple, with a small penknife. He
says,

'In those days, there were only thirty-two
households. Two families were middle peasants,
the others poor peasants, beggars who wandered
here and there, for food.'

(Behind the rustling awning: doors unbolted, deep under bulb-
light in their hillside; a dark catacomb, a storage-chamber of
apples, cascade and tonnage staved-off, and held up, by worn
matting, roped to wooden stakes, rammed into the tunnelled
ground.)

He spits peel into the palm of his hand, munching open-
mouthed.

'They had a poor and miserable life.
Their existence was not secure. After
today's meal, they did not know where
tomorrow's meal could come from. At
liberation, only two cows, two donkeys,
and one pig, were left.'

He pours the cold tea away on the earth-floor, and puts
away his penknife, raising the flap of his padded jacket, to
get at a pocket. Outside, (sheep bleating on the hillside), a
horse bares its teeth in a grimace.

In the apple-store, behind closed doors, the blood turning
cold, and the head heavy with fragrance, is a chilling clear
perfume beyond any mistaking, your life on ice, frozen.

69

Her shy, hesitating movement is beyond recalling. She is
startled to flushing (shared without motion, or stirring) at the
sound, akin to silence, of her own lightly-held breathing, or
the rustle of her clothing.

Around her, in the small half-dark cave-house, deepening
dark at the cave-end, and simple as sand, are great earthen
storage-jars, sets of timpani at the cave-wall, bamboo-lidded.
Her old worn hands falter (a tentative touching for something
to do, at the moment of your watching), or hover at the rim
of the stone-oven beside her. This caught blinking of the eyelid, a twinkling, is speaking's surrogate, and touching.

She has bound feet, and pin-pricked pierced ears; her cheeks
pink, to see the glancing at the raised platform in the cave-rear,
matting-covered for sleeping, blankets stacked and folded.
Pride has both a motion, and a resonance; and sounds well in
such a hillside. Smiling breaks the silence, and there is light
also, at the paper-windows.

All the lineaments of conversation, beyond first words and
introductions, are in the showings of her red-painted wooden
tray and eating-bowls, hanging metal-utensils strung swinging
on a wire; and two chests on trestles, covered in dark-woven
fibrous matting.

There are whole sentences in a cluster of wicker-baskets,
standing on ground swept and weathered, or in two nested
wooden-buckets, and a broom in the corner; and metaphors
for all the world, (life emptying, and soaring), in fingers fumbl-
ing to lift the bamboo-lids covering her stores of millet, and

her salted aromatic of vegetables, steeping in liquid for the winter, beyond any mere describing.

The holding of her sewing and stitching, lifted (black hair neat in a bun, with a net over it) from a chest on a trestle, is a sharing of life-work; her absent touching of the neat cluster of brushwood and stacked kindling, at the doorway, is all valediction.

70

In a dull Yenan room, is a restless person, a Yenan dancer, with delicate hands, sitting bolt upright in a dancer's posing, (feet crossed, in a frozen entrechat). Now, she crouches forward with her hands clasped (fingers entwined) between her knees; now sits back, with tapered fingers tautly-spread on her thigh, and (rocking to and fro, to unheard music) with fine figures of her wrists and fingers, fine poses, speaks of dancing. She says, en passant,

> "Massive activities of entertainment
> also unfolded, at the time of liberation",

and says, lightly smiling, (eyes shining),

> "Singing and dancing are a component
> part of a revolution."

The smell of smoke reaches into this room, also.

Though there is a pall, hanging still, over the grey Yenan pagoda, and the harsh concrete river-bridge; though these are no distant enchantments (as seen roseate, or gilded, or set among verdure, in posters and ideal visions of the 'sacred centre of the revolution'), coming down from the hill-villages, from such steep caves and fair blossoms, is no falling from a height. For these are iron positions, taken up on ground hard as war. In the stone-bouldered valley, where there are soldiers (washing their clothes in the Yenho river) at rifle-and-cannon-practice, in ranks of gunfire, down-to-earth, and lying in sand, hammered metal smiting at the centre of targets, there is no avoiding the ambush of smoke and iron in the air; no room for your manoeuvre, nor listless withdrawal.

These are passions, watching children running from a court-yard, squealing and squeaking, going indoors out of the dust. The courtyard is deserted, but the sand (stirred-up, pummelled, and trodden underfoot), still contains the childish agitation. In the silence of regret and concentration, there are voices, and even singing.

In the abbreviated moments of wandering, waiting to leave, there are last longings for the slow-moving tide, and street-press, of mountainous dark people, (men smoking from long pipes, crouching); drifting, in old stores leaning like grey wood-sheds, jostling and buffeted, at the blockaded drab doorways made shapeless by a multitude of rubbings and meetings; passing squat old buildings of patchings and shorings, shaken and bombarded in the barrage of armies, and old invasions (Yenan held, lost, recaptured); or sinking, amid quarry-blasts and stone-dust, into a ramshackle heavy darkness, walls peeling with posters.

Over the Shensi hills (bellows blowing deep in a dust-storm), a young army-girl stands in the tiny plane's gangway, holding on in the air, singing pink-faced, and swaying, hands clutching the seat-edge, finger-tips (here) before you, strands of hair by her cheeks. She sings as she speaks, and speaks as she sings,

and says only, in a child's giggling, 'Music must serve the
people.'

Pauperized and isolated by taut speculation, privacies, and
personal sinkings, embarrassed by a fever of vain misgivings,
face-to-face (and lost) with such feelings, you must put it
(scribbled in the shelter of cupped-hands, and your own note-
book) here, to remember the decisive moment's passing.

71

From the carriage-window, are fortresses and castle-keeps
of the imagination, beyond the leaves of a potted geranium,
flute-music, and a metal railway-soprano, crossing China and
boiling with passions. This is a boy's view, from a caterpillar
train, inserting itself through a gorge, and slithering down the
tiered green fields, set sheer among castellated sandstone, into
the plains of Hunan province. The crenellated sandstone-
terracing declines to a mere cliff-edge, just steep sand-hills
grooved and caverned among the green plateaus; tumuli and
conical ant-heaps of sand standing in green wheat, and yellow
rape-fields. These are no more than a child's sandcastles tunnelled with spades, hollowed and fallen, and too shallow for
a burrow; (the children themselves, with buckets and baskets,
are picking weeds on the sloping, passing, embankment, and
waving brushes). You can slide (this way) right down, to the
pink-grey, clay-smooth walled and wattled villages in the low-
lands (hills faded to pink, and red-brown, masses), clustered
in green; sandy houses, with roof-tiles upturning, beside the
grass-tufted, pitted, low walls of gullies; where, by the pink-
white dusty paths of early summer, pink-and-white trees in
blossom, there are small children dabbling and idling, fiddling
their fingers in water, and slippery summer-boys bathing
naked, deep in a narrow channel.

But an ageing woman, changing at noon, is at no child's play. With black peasant work-jacket opened on a mother's breasts, sweated naked body no object, and not startled, stopped for a moment under a hat of straw-yellow, slowly buttoning the clean work-shirt, and back bending in a fresh effort, she stoops in sunlight in a dug-field, red flags planted, heads hanging over the furrows.

72

In the heat of the open fields, or by the track's black metallic line, after eating, under tents of thin branches and wigwams of railway-sleepers, hung with matting, woven against the sun, men are curled up on their sides, sleeping. In the heat, a woman sitting in a handcart is pulled by a boy, into the shiny distance.

Among the men, women, children, oxen, horses, ponies, mules and asses carting, tugging and trudging, singly and in teams, laden cartwheels turning over the ground, are postures and passing gestures (a girl emptying her nostril, and, her cart driven to a standstill for your level-crossing, looking round at your black-bearded head, passing in the window) beyond all counting, or recounting:

> O, what shall you say of the boy down the
> lane, carrying a kid in his arms, and a white
> goat kicking up dust and following him,
> anxious, mouthing for a second at the·crook
> of his elbow?

> Or of the thin donkey's back-legs (moving
> quickly by), strained and buckling, hoofing
> there and foundering, huge grey cart tilted

back, and down, beyond budging under its
groaning load, beam-end grinding the ground,
whipped sitting, bucking and struggling, and
now hoisted; suddenly freed, the load launched
forward in sight, set lurching, and gone down
the track, in a twinkling?

In the day's slow wearing-down of thousands-upon-thousands
working, the sun becomes a grey disk for evening. Men and
women are washing clothes in the fields' passing channels,
pushing and pounding cloth mounds against stone, at the rim
of the water, the sun sinking.

People and animals are walking home to the day's end,
mules and ponies laden and knowing the way, looking round,
staring. In the dusk (falling slowly), light is drawn and gathered;
from mass steady motion to a clay-house, and a grey handcart.

73

A cook in a railway-apron stands at the night's crumpled
table-linen, beside the stacked and rattling dishes. Her eyes
are dark-shadowed by night-light, and long cooking, her face
shined by galley-heat, and hurry. She sings, against the racket-
ing over rail-lengths, and the hollow-clatter-over-bridges, plump
cheeks flushing. Pale men and women, cooks and guards, at
the hatches, in gangways (girls holding hands against wrong
notes, or drying), listen hard to her singing. But this 'Red
Detachment of Women' is a martial music, for blazing eye
and a bold spirit. There is a moment of discord, in such mopping of brows, glances and smiling.

Stopping, to a dying motion; and a long waiting in a black-out of creaking metal. The yellow unblinking eye has only its black and glassy reflections to go on, or the ear's contractions in a welling silence. There is a dead tapping of wheels. Someone is at the underbelly in an uncoupling of iron, faces and forms passing the motionless window. Outside (in humid night-heat at Chengchow Station), great red wheels of steam-locomotives are rolling slowly from sidings, towards the stopped and dusty sleeping wagons. A stoker, in the yellow-painted cab, leans gleaming out of sleep and a fiery-bright inferno. On the dark deserted platform, are stockpiles of concrete, standing in stifling blackness. There are columns of sleepers, dozing, or eyeless in the yawning silence.

The mind before dawn is unlit; idly alights, and rises again to a freezing stricken recognition: ON THE LONG DAWNING ROADWAY AND DISTANT EMBANKMENT, THERE ARE TWO ROLLING BATTLE-LINES, RED FLAGS FLYING, TWIN COLUMNS RUNNING EMPTY AND LOADED BY THE THOUSAND, IN PROCESSION, A GREY-UPON-GREY MOTION OF CARTS FAST PASSING IN THE NEAR-DARK, TO-AND-FROM SOME NEARING EPICENTRE, CART-SHAFTS PULLED AT THE WAIST, A WOMAN'S KNEES QUICKLY BENDING INTO DARKNESS, SETTING THE SHAFTS DOWN LIGHTLY, MEN AND WOMEN SPADING AND LOADING AT A SEETHING BANKED-EARTH MOUNTAIN AND MOLE-HILLS HALF-EATEN, CARTS LOADING IN THE FIRST-LIGHT, A SPADE FLUNG BY A GIRL IN A FLURRY ON A LOAD, LIFTING, SETTING OFF, PASSING AN ARRIVAL, PULLING AWAY, CRANING TO LOOK BACK, FAST AND GONE; AND, COMING-AND-GOING FROM THIS DIRECTION ALSO, A SECOND DOUBLE-COLUMN, STREAMING IN THOUSANDS TO-AND-FROM THE DIGGING, OVERTAKING A MULTITUDE JOINED FIGHTING EARTH AND MUD, IN THE STILL-DEAD EARLY MORNING, CARTS, AND MORE CARTS, PASSING AND RE-PASSING; the lines turning aside, and the carts moving away ; in the grey stillness, before sunrise.

With the sun-rise, thought touches upon a pyramid-tip somewhere, built to a height to stagger a pharaoh.

74

These are the old villages of an early-summer morning, cool behind window-glass, and beyond all reach.

There are men and women squatting in a cluster, beneath dark trees in a deep-purple flowering, eating from bowls before the day's up, lost and gone.

Only the eye-sight may touch such thatched houses, grey- or pink-plastered under green trees, marooned by the water-channels, by ponds mantled and standing; gone now also, surfaces beyond any ruffling.

There are long-poled black punts, tethered (and never to be seen untethered) at a green bank-side. But the white duck is in his dominion, coolly beaking and sifting through the water, unhurried, but snatched into the devouring distance.

Not even grey roofs, upturned with grey-brick toothed-tiling at the roof-corners, to repel evil spirits, will give a man any hand-hold, flying so.

You are not leaving, but left behind by, the tail of this passing single-file, walking and ducking under green leaves, spades and hoes moving along a green embankment, towards the water-meadows, and fields beyond a village.

Stopped in longing, at mid-morning; the fields are full, water-buffalo breasting the water of rice-paddies, the village unstirring. There are small heaps of building-materials (here) on a sandy pathway, covered by yellow woven-matting. An old limping man is pulling at the branch of an osier. He may be seeking a switch for a young man's fancied striding, but lets it go, breaking-off from failure. The old woman, plaiting and winding the soles of a rope-soled sandal, is also concentrated beyond any beckoning. There is only a scarecrow standing there in a peasant's straw-hat; while a flapping crow with a white head, comes down to a two-footed landing, finding his feet, and a firm grounding, folding his wings into order.

Earth breast-mounds are nippled with clay-bowls and clay-cups. These are old grave burials in the dotted (and dead-marked) green landscape, cones and beehives of the dead, standing their clay ground, and ploughed around. Green-growing wheat, rape-fields, the man and the ox, all stop and step round these mole-mounds. Some clay bowls tipping their swept hives, are tended and fluttering with thin white pennants, paper-tickets of memorial, fixed on the mound-sides. But other urns are tufted and grass-filled like birds' nests, molehills overgrown and grass-covered, sinking and decomposed, washed away by rains, and forgotten.

They have sunk to no more than a mid-field sand-pie, urn-less, but they are avoided by every plough and harrow, or ox-step.

75

A thundering crossing of the Yangtze, bellying junk-sails
far below in shining water, sets you down in summer-avenues
of full-leaved plane-trees, dragging carts, Nanking town-crowds,
evergreens in sand, and orange flowers. There are spreading
branches, vegetables hung (green and drying) on clothes-lines,
and women squatting at the road-side, open-legged, talking.
A soldier, carrying parcels, drops one, and bending to pick it
up, drops another. Here comes a man, and next a child, to
help him; three, bending together.

Fine mesh is cast, at a jetty, netting and riddling the water,
and sinking in a billow. Hoisted onto the straw-flecked and
worn river-bank, nets stand, large as jibs or spinnakers,
umbrella-spined, curved by the net-weight, raised on dry
ground and standing like umbrellas (open-to-dry after a shower
and resting on a beaked-handle and rib-end of a rib-cage),
heavy ferries and river-boats passing in a rocking wash, funnels
smoking.

This deep, sand-coloured, sunny water which you are looking at, is ribbed and ruffled by a warm blown wind. The sun is
steeping the river-banks, shimmering. And, down among the
Nanking wharves, the chimneys and the cargoes, the sun catches
a glinting warehouse-window, closing your eye. The sun warms
the weathered-grey junk sail-cloth, furling quietly down-wind;
warms the boatmen's backs, three standing bending to an oar,
leaning now to their slow forward-stroking, and poleing. Such
dipping and creaking, breeze-cupped, splashes in silence on the
ear. Worn-grey wooden boxes, loaded in open holds, or stacked like junk on the barge-decks (clothes strung hanging to dry,
at a wheel-house), move slowly down-river, sails and shirt-tails
slapping in a cross-current.

A child, perched at a boat's rim and nearest to the row-lock, is pushing on an oar, the oar rising over his dark head, its full height within reach only of a man, standing against the sun and thrusting forward at the oar's end, a woman in the middle. These three, standing, bending slowly to an oar, pass below you between the bridge-girders, also moving in the tide's flowing.

A lard Mao-mammoth stands in a cold marble hall at the bridge's mid-point, high above the river. The glacial floors, slippery and awash with mopping, are steep-banked with plastic roses and plastic chrysanthemums, sprayed for a scent, and in full plastic bloom; garden-flowers, turned by a Gorgon-Mao to stone. These flowers are death-stalked. Here, the concrete mountains and iron tonnage were poured into the fathoms, by fifty-thousand builders, streaming and diving from all-China to bridge the Yangtze.

Black leviathan-locomotives, red-emblazoned and fiery, roar across the shuddering river; in the silent aftermath, comes a pulled cart, shoulder-strapped and dragged creaking, the sound of lapping yawning below the macadam.

Set on the rail-and-road bridge's gigantic girders over the brown water, and over the huddled river-bank hutches (in the looming shadows of the black-webbed hatchings of iron), are nine-times-seven-ton red-iron sledge-hammers, giant characters:

'LONG LIVE CHAIRMAN MAO!'

in an heroic elephantiasis, heavy engineering fairy-lit for the hot night-time.

76

Knifed by the heat.

The room is blackened by the glaze.

The man and the child are sitting at the table.

There are other children playing outside, in the razor-glitter; hair haloed.

> '(smiling) Children used to compare their
> hands, to see whose were most white and tender.'

The small girl, legs fidgeting at the edge of the chair, is folding and kneading her handkerchief into a roll, eyes blinking.

He speaks softly in the heat, and near to a whisper. The windows are wide open.

> 'Now, they compare themselves by seeing
> who has the foremost ideas about physical
> labour.'

Gazing at his well-kept fine finger-nail touching the table, your eye narrows to a dazed pin-point.

> '(slowly) With their books in their
> hands, they spoke of marks only, just
> reading or reciting texts, learning them
> by heart, and not knowing their meaning.'

This is a silence of heat-loss, and shrinking. His face is pallid, his forehead shining. His shirt is open at the collar, to the adam's apple. The small girl moves a strand of hair from her face.

> '(quicker) I pay attention to the
> ideological education of my children,
> since this is the new revolutionary
> generation. Not taking part in physical
> labour, is regarded with shame. I say,
> even with education you must not become
> proud, nor look down on physical labour.
> (after a pause) When they come from
> school, I give them jobs which are in
> their power.'

The beady-eyed child, collects herself and sits upright, dwarf-ed, agog; feet not reaching the ground.

Then, he said, swallowing drily :

> 'My father was illiterate, and for forty-
> five years worked as a cleaner. He paid
> no attention to my education. He only
> wanted more children, so that, in old
> age, he could be looked after. My mother
> sent me to school, for six years of a
> Confucian education. To find out about
> me, she used to peep through the school-
> windows. I counted on my fingers, and
> with beans I brought from home. They
> only had two bowls of food for them-
> selves, each day. Today I am a clerk.
> Now, children like my own know
> many things, like the reasons for our
> struggle.'

The small girl's plaits are tied with green ribbon; listening.

'But children are no longer the property
of their parents. What they become
depends on them, not me. Yet, they will
serve the cause of the people.'

The short sleeves of her white-cotton shirt are creased. She
wears a brown-leather belt, and trousers. Pulses bobbing, fluttering and bursting, she says:

' I like best class-teaching, and activities
in political thought. I have most difficulties
with physical education. Games help us
morally, educationally and politically, but
I cannot run so fast.'

She folds the handkerchief into a sausage.

'I enjoy myself in the parks, and go to
films and dancing-dramas. I like especially
"The Red Lantern" and "The Red Detachment
of Women"'.

She straightens the tail of the sausage.

'Their political content is very good in
all respects.'

He said, sweating, softly:

'My son's characters, however, are so
small that you could not read them.
With his small characters, I saw that he

was influenced by me. I told him, I
write like this because I take notes.
(laughing swiftly, in the shadow) I
told him, you are a pupil and should
write larger.'

A silence, heat-struck. 'Thus from concrete practice, we
can analyse errors.'

A silence, the children of Los, playing. 'When they play
more than they study, I tell them of the bitter times.'

The trees are weighed down, loaded.

The blue sky is heavy, turning purple.

77

Cicadas roar. This is the resin and semen of Nanking summer.
Faience roofs hover above the trees, and blaze, reeling. The
screaming-pitch of cicadas in heat lifts heads to the height of
the creaking trees, the sandy road's deep-winding through
woods, staggered, far below. The crowds are sauntering, steeped in the sun's aroma.

Leaning head-first, and elbow-to-elbow, into the cool wall
of a marble tomb, blue crowds, milling and smiling, are gazing
into the eyes of primulas, in the slippered dark of a mausoleum,
a catholic fragrance. Outside, pavillion-roofs and pagodas are

dazzling, in flames. In the dark chamber is a shining-white sarcophagus, lines of trousers and feet at the altar-railing, and the last (stepped) ledge of marble. Outside, pines stand in roaring silence, rigid under such fire. The sculpted death-mask of the Manchus' deposer, Sun Yat-Sen, buried in high gothic pomp before a revolution, reposes in the marble of an old whispering religion. Outside, (higher), is the low heavy sighing, and soughing, of old forests, of towering timber, soaring; of the head's thunder. The day has fainted under the weight of this heat.

At the topmost balustrade of a pagoda-tower, dragonflies are circling, trembling (but not in terror), striped-black and grey-yellow; come closer, sun hovering on their honey-wings, darting and coming closer, but beyond all reaching.

In early evening sunlight, a field turns to a still meadow, a grove to an orchard. Here are violets and vetches, waiting; aconite and peach-blossom, made motionless and perfect at sundown. There are plane-trees shining by the cobbled country road. Children are climbing on the backs of a grey avenue of standing, and couched, stone-lions and camels. Birds are singing to the failing light, bruising for thunder.

The curtains are stirring. A door bangs in a gust of wind. Outside, dust is swirling into the eyes. Great rumbling gusts of rain fall on beds of marigold, and bamboo. A window and a shutter are wrenched and flung by wind, glass breaking. In a flash of lightning, there are men, women and children, foreheads glistening, and soldiers, ushering and scurrying against the storm's rising. There is a chemical smell of damp on dry dust, and thunder collapsing. The trees are buckling, arms waving, hair streaming, sheeted with rain.

The sky cracks open.

78

Here (in motion), the doors of houses are open. A man stands in a small dawn pool, limpid as an eye-ball, washing his feet, white ducks walking (heads erect, looking around them). There are two rubber-boots lying on the ground, behind him. A man, pencilled at a pond-edge, fishes the still water, thin rod-tip and fine surface fragile as an outline, slight as the batting of an eyelid.

Dark pools, deep in reeds and screened by rail-glass, (begonia-flowers trembling, in a delicate vibration at the table), stand mirror-still, or drifting with early mist.

Here (in motion), there are buffaloes sheltering, heads tethered and lowered, holding still. The calm wreathed hills are snuffed-out, swaddled in fallen clouds. Animals stand, subdued, under dripping thatch-awnings. Their carts are waiting in a clearing, bowed in steady rain, or kneeling.

The rain is thinning and stilling, the trees veiled to greyness, in a soft motionless falling. A girl, holding a small enamel-bowl in her hand and standing (legs apart), cranes forward, brushing her teeth. There are white spittings, on ground blackened by rain, between her feet.

It is drizzling, fine as a fountain mist, on planted paddies, asprout with fingers of pale green, in water. Along the spider-thin paths, and grey-bridged webs of water, men and women are setting off to water-green fields, past green osiers and limp bamboo; a mushrooming along bubbled wet paths, under brown umbrellas.

The slow grey water-buffalo plods elephantine, in a cloud; rider stately as in a howdah, bare legs against heaving wet flanks, a faint spray splashed from heavy hooves, planted softly, under water.

The splashing road to Ci Xia Shan is glistening black, under hanging rain, a lake asphalt, gleaming yellow umbrellas in full-sail, to school.

An old man, with a crouching squat gait, bent over a stick, walks quick and bald into a courtyard, holding a bowl clamped to his hand. A woman stoops (out in the open), awash in muddy water, beating a roll of clothes with a thick stick. Burial mounds stand like kilns, sinking in flat river-land. The haystacks are straw-hatted, and top-knotted with plaitings. A heavy-jowled black mongrel, champing at the bit, pads along a bank ridge, dew-laps to the trail, breaking into a bounding run, box-headed. A grey petrified lion stands up suddenly, in a green field, tail curling and turning over its dark wet haunches, smiling at such lushness. The morning rises to full day-light, and the rain's last wringings.

Standing in punts, men and women are scooping up river-mud, with long-poled ladles, tipping and heaping it on the banking; shovelling, spading, loading and lifting it onto shoulders; tripping sideways, balancing on a tight-rope, (a man in a straw hat, squatting on the roof of a box-beehive, looking down at the bees' swarming), with poles at their shoulders; carrying, in suspension, baskets of mud, and buckets of water, stopping, adjusting the weight, splashing it into balance, and running in single files along footprint-wide ridges;

stooping and bending in straw-hats, trousers rolled to the knee, standing in fields of growing wheat, rice, rape, beans, and clover; raising large-toothed rakes, up in the rainy air and down, steady, shirts lifting and pulling across chests and falling; young women with long-plaited hair and patched trousers, upright and leaning slowly forward, hips swivelling and hoeing in purple clover; a jerusalem and gigantic rhythm of arms and bodies in movement, of patched and pieced clothing, of blues washed and faded to their last grey frayings, and washed-out in this watery sunlight.

Sails are moving to Shanghai in river-land fields of wheat, junks anchored at the racing furrow-ends.

The train swerves by the curving village calligraphy, the raised eye-brows and black strokes of exclamation (on white-wash) of 'NIGHT-SOIL FORBIDDEN TO BE PLACED HERE!!!'

Villages (in fast motion) crowd the river-banks, the canal-ways quickly narrowing, and humped-over with bridges.

The land surrenders to the city.

79

At the very moment of your entry through the needle-eye of the last tunnel-darkness before the city, a man stood in muddied preoccupation at a cart-wheel, by the water's rim, shading his eyes to see you, speeding.

This fast deceleration, past walls and through Shanghai

streets to a standstill, discharges dense energy into an explosion of crowds and station-banks of flowers, metal-braking and singing in a hiss of steam. Concentration bursts out of focus in the turbulence of cavernous Shanghai canyons, in the swirling and hurrying cross-currents of thousands, in a downtown coursing through the great city, purged by a blood-change, and overhung with a massive roaring of political war-cries to the liberation of all peoples.

(At a raging corner, a soldier on point-duty whistles and gestures to a cyclist, to stop for a traffic-light. The cyclist looks round, and pedals on, faster.)

Funnelling down arterial avenues of the old-colons' grey-granite banking-palaces, passing glass-frontages bulging with the merchandise of a new epoch, treading through narrower (cleaned-out) depths (no gold, no bars) and into walled-in defiles, now clarified of old sufferings and jingling with bells, the free-wheeling mass-motion is reduced to twin files in an alley, buoyed-up, and shoulder-to-shoulder.

At the river's edge, is an open blowing, and a rusting tonnage, sucking, riding heavily at anchor. These are the roads of the sea-going river. Deep in this gleaming water are giants on the tide; and, in the stiff sea-breeze, steamer-sirens on the wing.

The junks are bucking and chopping through this juggling water, the barges near-foundering in their own furrows. There carries here the sound (and drift) of millions: river-sirens, rung bells, and turning wheels, the movements and launchings of an oceanic city. The gantries roll, rumbling, in a heavy haulage, above the steady surge of crowds.

Later, in the humid and misty night, the long-deserted sea-streets are wet with damp. There are small points of light on the river, a searchlight in the black ripples, and a red-neon eye on the warehouse-roof. A ship at the river-bar has weighed anchor, and is sailing through the mists of wailing, and sea-shrouds. You came to this river-wall too late to catch the turning of the tide, this Chinese sea-change.

80

Here is a small boy to take your hand.

Children are running up-and-down stairs to work-rooms, or out into the open.

There is a small round-dance of children, on the sunny grass.

"In this Palace of Children teachers, workers, and retired people teach their skills to the children, in their spare-hours. (a door banging) Here, we put proletarian politics in command, organizing activities for the moral, physical and intellectual development of the children. (children fidgeting) Here, old workers come to tell the stories of their sufferings to the children, to make them more politically conscious. (a distant siren) We must also let our children know the ways of life of foreign lands, so that they may learn

of the sufferings of the labouring
people the world over."

Children are listening, two to a chair; or, sitting on the
knees of other children; or, in the laps of teachers and old
people, folded in arms.

In a room, a young girl needles her own leg, at the calf,
a mechanic pointing to a wall-chart of her nerve-ends. In
another, small girls pirouette, or stand on points, (held at
the waist by puffed boys.) A teacher making an electric-bell
staunches the ringing with her fingers. This room clanks with
pestles in mortars. At a corridor's end, hands shaking in din,
an old printer sets a machine rolling and printing, boys'
hands diving and scooping paper, to a shouted explanation.

You may look round these doors at children's open-mouthed
singing; at a girl putting two folded cotton-jackets on to a
stool, and sitting down at the piano, into a room quivering
with violinists; at scissors, clipping paper-cuts (tongue-tips
between teeth, for precision, and river-echoes between the
breath and the silence), at ink and paint, carefully exploding
in a people's water-coloured war, on paper.

A door opens on an electrician, glueing a balsa tail-plane,
in a press of children on tip-toe.

81

In a cul-de-sac of peering exhibition-crowds, and standing
on a platform of light veneer, are shiny bicycles smelling new,

strong as hardened steel (in the racks and spokes) for heavy-
weights, and sackloads;

operation-beds, folded down into boxes, for barefoot-doctors
to carry in the country-side;

saddles, mounted on frames and bolted to the floor, for
stationary cyclists, pedalling hard, to make the light shine;

and, shirts and vests, thick-sewn at the shoulders, for the
rubbing rope, heaving at the cart-wheel.

In a marbled medical-annexe, severed fingers (re-sewn and
dark-blue with scars) pluck apples from the pictured bough;
on silent film, hearts bleed, and stomachs open in a gush, on
show. Screen arms are needled. mouth-masked heads bending
over an abdomen, eyes glancing over the gagging, patient foreheads shining under arc-lights, in the sweat of a crisis. Lips
part for orange slivers, fingered by hands in stretched rubber.
There is a sucking and smiling, as the celluloid knife plunges.
After the stitching, acupunctured men sit up from their death-
beds, nodding.

Girls' arms point, in the slow hum of the juggernaut-machine,
to exhibited metal. The gothic generator-halls of chandeliers
and marble are flag-hung; a mass, weighted to the ground.

    'The girls who explain the exhibits, are
    the workers of the young generation,
    learning while they work. Otherwise,
    they would know only their own jobs.
    Children who come here ask questions
    of the workers, who have actually made
    the exhibits. Thus, we can learn from

each other, gather the fruits of
initiative and self-reliance, and see
what can be done.'

Girls' slippered feet are planted on stands, weight at the
waist pressed against cold-drawn guard-rails. Furnaces and
free-forging presses stand jacked-up, in a gleaming dead-weight
of huge hydraulics. Banked and winking electonics, and whirring turbines, large as locomotives, are moored (in elephant-
grey gun-metal) to the marble ground.

Machine-tools rotor the water-cooled metal. Thread-grind-
ing turns milky, rippling grey behind panels, port-holes in
iron. Laser wave-lengths cut metal to silence, hands raised to
mouths.

And, at the summit of a dripping mountain-torrent of
green-jade candlewax, in a display-case, a Red Flag is planted.
The crowd, padding and soft-footed, strolls and saunters,
plaited arm-in-arm, or hands in pockets.

82

Light-green ferries, sound-waves silenced by distance, are
crossing the muddy-brown Shanghai city-river, smoke-stacks
blackened. Junks catch the wind's turning in silence. They
soar, moving into light, flying in full-sail. Over-loaded barges,
tugged and towed low in the tide, or under their own steam,
move slowly in progress up-river, wallowing in travail, or treading water.

A deck-hand moves down-stream, high at a rail sliding to

sea, the tide making light of his labour. He bends, swabbing
down the decks, swilling and flushing in a spray of hose-water.

83

They sit down on faded brown-leather sofas, taking up
positions, coughing in the hollow room, and speaking sidelong into ears, spittoons and boots placed carefully on worn-
dull factory carpets. Outside, men in work-clothes and caps
cross to and fro, past the metal-frame windows; hard labour
and concrete action in dead earnest, and a greying wind. Doors
slam, the glass-reflections of caps and foreheads in the Mao-
portrait tipping, and trembling. There is a coming to order, a
spitting and thudding.

      (speaking into noise) 'Here used to be
      merely low houses, made of iron sheets.
      Before liberation, hoes and rakes only
      were made, simple farm-tools,'

fists pouring tea, matches flaring.

      (gaining ground) 'In revolution, we
      severely repudiated the philosophy of the
      slavish comprador, turning anger into
      strength, and a soaring spirit.'

There is a coughing to silence, hands rubbing. A late-comer
crosses the threadbare carpet, shoes in a hurry.

      (and settling into stride) 'Indignation
      turned to effort. We threw ourselves,
      heart-and-soul, into the struggle to grasp

revolution, and to promote production.
We repudiated decisively the doctrine of
trailing-behind, poor-and-blank, at a
snail's-pace!'

A khaki-cap leans back in an armchair, knees crossing,
eyes blinking against a smoke-cloud, face in a muscling movement, at the jaw; amid the settled smoking.

A sallow voice rises under a cap.

(insisting) 'We transformed production,
by hard-struggle, while maintaining our
independence. We kept initiative in our
own hands, and relied on our own efforts!
(loudly) We concentrated the wisdom and
experience of the masses, and smashed all
time-worn conventions!! (whisperings in
the room, and tea-sipping) We broadened
the technical ranks of the working-class,
bringing our skills into full play. (voices,
passing the window) We finally solved the
key-problems of the construction of
forty-ton machine-tools, (tea-mugs
rattling) not with huge equipment, not
with big technical resources, but (quickly,
casually) with the power of proletarian
engineering.'

There is a stirring of feet on the carpet, and the sounds of
marshalling-yards, waggons shunting iron-upon-iron, at junct-
ions.

Laddered chimneys funnel blackness, high, over the long barrack-workshops and warehouse-roofing, into the sky-line. A light lattice and scaffold of cat-walks, (and hand-rails), laces-up the heaped barrage-blocks of grey-sloping hangars, silhouettes walking the gang-planks.

There are feet scuffling; tea-lids lifted, and supping.

(slowly) 'Our great leader Chairman Mao said to the masses of China, when he personally inspected this plant, on July 8, 1957. 'PUT PROLETARIAN POLITICS IN COMMAND, AND TAKE THE ROAD OF THE SHANGHAI MACHINE-TOOL PLANT, IN TRAINING TECHNICIANS FROM AMONG THE WORKERS!!: (slowly) Practice proves that, in this way, the political consciousness of the broad-masses will be raised. (slowly) The workers will become master of science, and technology, and production will promote the revolution!'

Beneath the streaming white shouts, swerving across red triumphal archways ('FACE UP TO ANY DIFFICULTY HOW-EVER GREAT!!'; 'TURN BAD THINGS INTO GOOD ONES!', 'SHANGHAI MACHINE TOOL PLANT IS FORGING AHEAD WITH GIANT CHANGES!!'), stragglers walk past thin factory-shrubs, and metal window-frames brown-painted in cream concrete; a flag and a lightning-conductor stand parallel on a roof-top.

Tea-mugs are topped-up, to brimming; mouths pursed, cupping and blowing.

'So, how did the sweeper Shou Kuei-Fu
become a technician? The older
technicians ridiculed him, saying
"Does the revolution mean that every
sweeper can become a technician?
This is just like crying for the moon!"'

Supping and whispering.

'They took a sceptical attitude to him.
When he encountered difficulties, he
went to an engineer. The latter knew
well that Shou Kuei-Fu did not understand English, but gave him an English
reference-book. Shou Kuei-Fu refused
to accept it.

The engineer said, "Since you don't
understand the ABC, how can you become
an engineer?". Shou replied, "I have
accumulated practical experience,
through my work."

The engineer replied. "But since you
also do not understand XYZ, you still
cannot become an engineer."'

Legs are crossed and re-crossed; a pale and diffident face
exhaling smoke, through flaring nostrils, one eye closed, and
hand on knee.

'Shou replied, "Our ancestors did not
know the ABC either, but they invented
many things. As for you, you may know
the ABC and the XYZ, but you are

divorced from the masses, and they will
despise you." Shou went away.

But he remembered that 'WITHOUT
CULTURE AN ARMY BECOMES A
FOOLISH ARMY'. So he studied hard
on his own, was sent to be trained as
a technician, by the vote of his comrades,
and mastered the ABC, and the XYZ.'

A haze of blue cigarette-smoke, the voice easing.

'Shou Kuei-Fu is now in charge of the
technical affairs of our plant. He
gained a high degree of political
consciousness, from his former
miserable life as a sweeper.'

Faces are nodding, eyes darting for recognition, the light
dying. Siren-clouds of white steam are puffing from flue-pipes,
or hissing and leaking from stadium-roof vents.

The yards and rope-walks are snaked with heavy cables,
and stacked with iron, gangers loading crated metal, at the
hangars' sliding-doorways; wheels slurring, in oil-caked and
blackened runners. Cleared gangways are over-hung by gantries
and heavy lifting-tackle, rolling along rails, pulley-blocks large-
as-anchors swinging idle. Labour-force, and oily hands (dark-
blue sleeves, and sleeve-cuffs, behind the perspex of plastic
arm-guards) plunge deep into serried metal, in the grey-girdered
arena, girls and men poised casual (or hands winching) at
vices, dark-blue mob-caps bending to grey lathes and gear-
levers; or, leaning over into the whirring bellies of cylinders,
in motion. Towels and flannels hang drying, on lines, strung

low at the work-bench, faces from the opera smiling ruddy, on whitewash. Blackboards are chalkmarked with red texts,

('THE BROAD MASSES ARE DETERMINED TO ADVANCE ALONG THE ROAD TO WORLD REVOLUTION WITH BIG AND STEADY STRIDES AND FLYING COLOURS!!'),

or pinned with posters of fists and spanners, young girls smiling, mouths opening, shrugging shoulders in the dinning rhythm. Beaming steel is precision-ground to a glassy mirror-finish under lamp-light ('to the adjacent pitch-error of only one twenty-fourth of a human hair's-breadth'), faces and caps silvered, sliced, rolled, and lengthened, to a long yawning (or squeezed laughter) in the mercury reflections of slipping and turning metal.

84

Hoarse-voiced, thin-faced, and pulling through a bleak fag, pointed nose turning straight and bony, he speaks quickly against the clock.

"I was born in a poor family. From the time my father was a child, he worked in a factory. My mother's life was bitter with sickness. If I tell the details, my eyes fill with tears."

There is unease, and shifting, in the dreary factory-room. He clips a puff from a drained cigarette, tilting his head, thin fingers stubbing in the ash-tray, setting his face to grimness.

"When I was a boy, I too had to go to the
factory. I could not have my own aims.
I was influenced by superstition that my
destiny was fixed, that I must work for
the exploiter. We worked cruelly, from
early morning to the late night. What
we ate each day, did not meet the loss
of our strength."

He looks away briefly, the dead bulb-light catching and
glazing his cheek-bone. His voice is suddenly on the rise, the
clock-hand moving a metal clank one-minute forward.

"Sometimes we just had wild-vegetables
to eat", rising to throttled pitch. "My
eldest sister and younger brother died
of disease. My uncle died of hard labour",
brush of hair bowing stiffly, gullet fluttering. "We had no money to buy a coffin
for him", Wu Tsao-Ken weeping. "His
corpse was eaten by dogs", a phone
ringing, shaking his head, as if puzzled.

Others look away, flushing; all ears on the phone's ringing.
The side of his head is cropped and grey-bristled, a long
curving and horned nail at his little finger-end, resting on his
large blue overalls.

He says, wiping his eyes with the back of his hand,

"When I think of this, my anger makes
me tremble."

A cigarette hangs in his fingers, body sidelong on the sofa, legs apart.

> "I was ill. We had no money for the doctor", strained fingers curled and gripping the sofa-seat, between his legs. "They kicked me out, saying, 'We will not allow this child to die, inside our factory.'"

Wu Tsao-Ken glances rapidly about him, turning head-on, his live-wired hair high-standing (and greying), sitting forward and slashing the air, breath on your face, the others looking cautiously towards him, askance, and away again, unstirring.

> "We suffered, though we struggled many times, because we were disunited. We struck often, but we had no strength! I was saved by liberation. I went to study. I learned to read and write. Then, I learned to understand the reasons for our poor living. I learned, that it was not fate which made the ignorance and hunger and the sufferings of the masses, but the exploiter. I was educated by the revolution."

The bare room sits blinking, unmoving. There is a silence of unmet glances. He sits back, withdrawing, distracted or intent; pursing his lips, as if smiling, or wincing.

198

85

There is a dark press pushing softly under the trees beside
the blackened Shanghai river, tar-black water (leaning over
into this styx, blinded) steep at the quays. Casual faces are lit
only in passing beneath wan lamp-light, the crowd, all blue
but blacked-out, moving in whispers, flowing along the water-
front, or standing at the river-wall, talking in low-pitched
voices.

Heavy faces, large and earnest; or, thin-boned and in pale
thought, eyes shining or laughing for a moment; beam briefly
into sight, pass and darken. Eyes, hollowed, are socketed
shadows, and open mouths black and yawning. The black mass
of backs and shoulders moves slowly along the river, talking.

Just here, in the leaden shuffle and passage of feet, and
the rustle and jostle of clothing, the dim light streams like a
soft fog through muffled branches. Youths stand speaking
together arm-in-arm, or in a huddle, bicycles propped under
the trees against the black flower-beds' stone-kerbing; or pass
through the heavy savour of night-damps in earth, brushing
past the low privet-hedges.

In the faint dawn from your bleary window, the roaring
posters are silent, the hoardings shut-down, red ardour doused,
and ashen.

Sun and light rise, and shine slanting on giant figures flexing their tumid muscle, billboard shoulders squared and braced
for fiery effort, shirt-sleeves big as junksails furled round blown-
up biceps. Thirty-feet from the ground, red mouths widen in
shouts of revolutionary triumph.

The green riverside gardens are quiet, and unfolding; cranes and barges at a standstill, misty water chopping and lapping. Two men are leaping and posing at an early morning sword-dance, silver-painted scabbards placed on the wet privet, at the gardens' rim.

Alone on a side-path, beside a yellow bed of soaked mari-golds, an old man is prancing slowly, arms rolling and folding. Two young men, arguing at the deserted river-wall, voices fresh and damped by morning, buck and bend, hands slapping to a fight, pushing, one snatching at the other's hair; then, pack it in, laughing and swaggering, and quickly cross the wide wet road into the city, walking lightly.

86

This is merely a cluster of huddled houses, and chimneys smoking in the fields.

The houses are thatched, or tiled, or slated.

The slates are dark-grey, the walls whitewashed.

Along the whitewashed walls, green vegetables are hanging to dry, on lines.

The day is grey-green.

You walk the cobbled streets, in well-being.

Barges are being punted through Nan-Shang hamlet, near Shanghai, in grey water.

There are wells in the courtyards, or stand-taps.

The houses are thinly timbered, grey and grey-black, with light bamboo-laths in plaster, some chimneys smoking.

This is the last journey into the country.

The grey-winding cobbled streets of low whitewashed houses, and the stone-flagged courtyards, are swept clean.

Old people are standing in doorways.

The barges move slowly, poled, loaded.

White ducks are backing, and paddling away in the water.

There are canvas-shoes and gloves pinned hanging on lines, drying.

A barefoot woman is squatting, and washing her shoes under a tap.

Wooden bowls are rinsing, vegetables being peeled at mid-morning in running water, a bucket handle clanking.

The small commune-office is lacquered red, with dark-red lattice-work, an old balcony, and a swept, cobbled, courtyard.

There are spring trees in the courtyard, their boles whitewashed.

The narrow grey canals are tree-lined, washing strung from trunk-to-trunk, or spread over green bushes.

The fields are deep in wheat and barley, waist-high, or flattened by rain; straw scarecrows standing, and women hoe-ing.

There is a smell of hay, thatch, smoke, hens, pigs, and green vegetables; hens stepping, and squawking.

A pig is being loaded onto a cart, squatting haunches prodded and pressed into a mesh-cage; frightened.

There are small haystacks in the village (children peeping between them).

In the commune-office, the colour of rosewood, the floor a dark red-brown timber, a thin young man, (with layers of pullovers beneath his blue jacket), warms his hands around a tea-mug, sitting at a long table covered with a dark-blue cotton cloth. His eyes blink into a blur of figures, in a clatter of cup-lids; a pen in his top-pocket. The girl who has served you tea wipes her mouth with a dark handkerchief, and disappears into a side-room.

At the end of cart-tracks (a hen pecking in the wheel-ruts) running deep between the barley, are chimneys, shovelling, and machines thumping, behind closed ramshackle doors. In the sudden dark, (going in), there is a blast of glowing orange fire, village-men's cheeks bulging in heat, blowing glass balloons through rod-tubes, rotated to a bulb-shape.

A woman, standing near the suddenly-opened doorway (turning quickly, blinking in the light, and holding a straw-fan in a gloved hand), darting in a hot fast flurry, lays onto bamboo-matting a billowy-thin glass-fibre, streaming from darkness to the doorway, runny and viscous as a syrup-thread; other padding feet are backing fast towards her, padded hands stretched-out with other threads, running the length of the workshop, to be laid hot, and in a hurry, on the bamboo-matting.

Or, there is a hot-tin smell of gas-jets on metal, heads bending under stand-lamps, in a tweezering and tinkling of filament-wire, fine as catgut.

In a plot of cabbage and spring-onions, at the foundry-wall, white butterflies flutter. A red flag blows over rusting metal, moulds, and mounds of coke-slack and slurry. Village foundry-men and -women stand deep in coke-dust, soft as powdered charcoal, in long peaked caps, flaps hanging down their shoulders, manhandling sledge-hammer tools, (grappled in gloves of heavy asbestos), bellowing in the furnace-roar, behind visors.

Girls are crouching in the near, still, fields; planting, in a mild spring breeze, for the summer.

There are sparrows twittering in straw.

Bamboo-matting and blankets, are airing; windows, open.

87

Two cheeping black chicks run about the uneven earth-floor. There is a smell of cooking, and rice boiling. In the other white-washed room, are a loom, and an old canopied bed, inlaid with mirrors, and painted with flowers and peacocks.

She stands up small, with short-cut hair, pouring cups of hot water from a flask, apple-russet face round, and wrinkled into a deep smile. She sits down again, hands folded at the table, smiling to you to drink the hot water.

The flask, with a bamboo handle, is covered in woven-straw plaitings, a string attached to its cork. A pot is steaming (the lid lifting) on the round clay-oven. Strings of millet are drying in lines along the whitewash. Clipped with bamboo-pegs, there also hang a basket-weave grain-riddle, a calendar, a stub of strung chalk, and, on a nail, a slate in a dark wooden frame; in a corner, are a bamboo crate, wicker-baskets, and a stack of dry branches.

She goes to take the pot off the fire, raising the lid in a cloud of steam.

Outside the door, there is a pair of frayed canvas-shoes, rope-soled, hoisted and drying on two bamboo sticks, stuck in the earth; beyond them, straw-silent, the cart-track.

88

A chain runs rattling over wood, into water. Grit is in your shoes, the toe-caps dusty. The sun comes out on the creaking of a barge, on wisps of straw, and coke, stacked on the tow-path. A hoarse voice in the silence talks softly on deck, under a bamboo-awning. Barefoot men run up planks, over the ripple of water, bricks suspended from shoulder-poles; and are stacked, clanking. The fields are deepest here, brick-kilns behind barley.

A small cheep, a muffled cock-crow, a crying or bleating, are spaced thin in stillness, or smothered in warm straw and sun-light; and, when stopped, they are imagined, the ears drumming.

A man and a small child are walking hand-in-hand, centred on a cart-track, slowly walking the long-drawn axis, between

fields. A barge rides at anchor on the waterway; a man in a
plot is bending to the ground.

There are people in a doorway, watching. Clothes are drying, wicker-baskets of pulled vegetables standing beside ruts
and straight furrows. The pads of a small dog along the beat-
en path are too light and quick to follow. Bristling and snub-
nosed, it runs softly to a man, a woman, and a child in arms,
snuffling the dust at their feet, in a passion.

There is a dense sweet smell of pigs and mulch under-foot
in a heavy silence, of animals munching or breathing thickly
in dark tetherings, and steaming fodder; coughing or stirring
in manure, or standing still, and waiting.

Stalks are stiffening rigid in an old shed, fragrant rape drying, bright yellow flowers upright, arrested and blazing in
the dark, dying leaves shrunken and withered.

A buffalo stands here, fixed pivot of a fleeting moment,
tethered to a stone, pent-up; an unblinking bull's-eye, and
a caked cart-axle, in the shudder of the world's slow turning.

Alone along the cart-track, given new sight and new sense,
you are knee-deep in fields of knowledge; all sound now
snuffed-out, for a heavy climax.

89

Now, go to the last warehouse-landing, up creaking and
worn stairs, sacks swinging down squeaking and heavy; your
fingers running along the dusty flutes and grooves of dark

window-ledges; stopping, time running out, and breathing a
cloudy blow-hole onto greying windows, over the cargoes
and the dry white-washed hosannas, pealing from the dock-
yard hoardings.

Sacks are squeaking down, quickly grabbed and grappled by
strong-arm squads, ham-fisted.

The obscure sofas are battered to dullness.

The dockers' chairman (in rimless glasses) sits down, squat,
to a heavy crouching, straddling the chair, jacket-sleeves riding
up the forearms, hands thick-set in a rough bunch at the table.

Under the stopped propellers of black fans, in bleaching
neon, stumping the dock-office's bareboards, pale girls and
plump women in blue caps, nodding and smiling, fresh-faced
or thin bespectacled men (tattered books, and an old globe
in the glass-fronted bookcase, overhung by Chairman Mao),
heavy men, burly necks bulging, or large-limbed with browned
teeth and lantern jaws, arms swinging, fill the thudding room.

Gripping the chair-arms and pushing himself forward, he
says,

> "We set up underground organizations in
> the Shanghai dockyards, and launched
> fierce struggles. We struck, again and
> again, stopped loading and unloading,
> occupying the docks, and pouring the
> heavy cargoes into the harbour."

Unravelling iron is dropping fast, grapnels swinging and

falling.

Voice moving briskly to a head, he says, setting-to,

> "When they surrounded the docks to force
> us to work, and used violence against us,
> we took up iron-bars, and attacked them,
> launching ferocious assaults on the
> police, turning over and burning the
> cars of the reactionary forces, and
> smashing everything to pieces";

head butting downwards,

> "So we learned that the oppressed and
> lowly must use armed force to seize
> power. We set out upon the long road to
> overthrow the overseers and to get power
> into our own hands, so that the dockers
> and coal-crushers could be master of
> this state."

Heavy chains are dragging their links into an iron coil;
cabled and crated freight is heaved up, swaying from crane-
jibs and skeleton-derricks.

> "Now, the struggles of the world's
> workers are our struggles; their
> victories are victories for the
> Chinese people. With organized
> struggle, no matter what the unity
> of the enemy, they are bound to be
> defeated."

Truck-loads of freight hang in the sky, rocking to and fro.

90

A small thin boy, grown past middle-age, with big ears and cropped hair, snub-nosed, high-chested and hard-breathing, taps the table with bony fingers.

> "I have been a docker for thirty years.
> We shouldered the cargoes from the boats.
> We moved the heavy sacks of rice and
> soda on our shoulders. Two-hundred
> catties each man carried, on his back;
> and on poles, pig-iron and girders. We
> did not have enough food, or clothing.
> We were not treated as men, but as
> draft-oxen and as beasts of burden."

Freighters, rope-laddered, cradled with wrist-thick cables and moorings, hung to iron-bollards, are docked, and discharging.

> "The docks were called hell on earth. We
> lived in the lower depths of hell. We had
> no right to speak, and died like our
> fathers, of cold and starvation. We slept
> in lavatories, and in the streets, in the
> doorways. There are eighteen floors
> of hell. We lived at the lowest level.
> All men oppressed us, the capitalist,
> the slavish comprador, and the reaction-
> ary classes. We were abused and beaten,
> because we had no political position.
> If there was a boat, they called us.
> There were few ships at the dock,
> but many workers in the streets,

waiting. Then, we were treated like
rags, and torn papers.''

Bilge-water is pumping from sterns into the dark harbour,
cranes dumping the wharves with cargo.

(Winded, taking breath) "There were
two failings; to be ill, and to get aged.
The strong and the solid-built, even
those who could carry four-hundred
catties, became weak and ill, and died
also, like the others.''

There is the sound of fork-lift trucks backing and braking;
going forward, and revving to a muffled thumping.

91

Listening ear-cupped, an ageing man places his swollen
fists on the table, body gawky and heaving.

"He could carry two sacks together, four-
hundred catties on his shoulder. Comrade
Hung was my friend, a strong person.
When we were young, they employed us;
O, when we were old, we were kicked away!!''

Standing up, voice and gesture break into a gaunt antiphon
rhythm. His arms scythe the time away, memory brought to
this hoarse dancing and livid smiling, a tall old man, lips blue
in the neon, in a slow chalky shouting, and swallowing.

"He drank water from the river, he had
cold cakes to eat only! His life was
cold, and became full of diseases!!
(voice bumping on stone) He was kicked
out in the roadway! Comrade Hung died
like a beast, in a doorway!!! Why could
he not keep his own living? Why did his
life have such an ending?"

His eyes have watered, his head stirring and startling, mouth
struck wide and heavy, garbled as with a cluttering of broken
teeth, fingers fitfully prodding the table.

Sacks hang, bulging in cradles and hammocks, swinging;
some trickling, and spilling.

Drawing himself up in a rage of lost words, and a dying
fall, sallow at the table, chin grey-stubbled, in blue overalls,
fingers stubbing and plucking at his chest, he rises to a croaking anger, voice blackening to its coda.

(extending his arms) "See! I was a
strong man, also!! I toiled all day,
but remained a beggar! I did not have
a family. I lived the years, in a lavatory!!"

The room balks, and backs away quietly.

His fingers rest hooked on his chest, not stirring, eyes
charging into silence. He touches his blue cap, subsiding,
leaden-grey hands trembling.

92

Tipping girders are handled (shouting and helmeted faces craning upwards) into empty drumming vessels, holds thudded and booming; are winched and hoisted by lifting-tackle, iron balanced, and floating in the air.

"Each day's work today, is equal to
forty days' work before liberation."

"We rebuilt the docks on the ruins
left by the reactionaries."

"We have built clinics and bathrooms,
nurseries and kindergartens, and
are realizing all-round mechanization."

"This was put forward by the cooks,
applying Chairman Mao's teachings, 'Let
us put the stress on the Four Warms!
Soup should be warm, meals should be
warm, dishes should be warm, hearts
should be warm!'"

"In this dock, two-thousand seven-
hundred men and women handle in one
year three-and-a-half million tons of
general goods, iron and steel, and
passengers for Dairen and Tsingtao."

Stepping round spars, cordage, and coiled chains along the crane-tracks; and the last ringing voices.

('INCREASES IN PRODUCTIVE FORCES, ON

SUCH A SCALE, ARE BASED NOT ON RAISED
INTENSITY OF LABOUR, BUT ON THE SEIZURE
OF STATE-POWER, AND THE MASS TRANS-
FORMATION OF ALL RELATIONS IN
PRODUCTION!')

There is a funnelled trumpeting, dry-blown and bellying,
(all stops pulled), into an organ-heavy diapason; and a crush-
ing siren-blast.

93

The mind turns away, looking down deep canyon-wharves,
stocked and crated; the room sinking into the wake, and dark
passage, of the siren's echo.

A slow and deep-toned voice (eyes composed and steady)
sets off to a conclusion.

> "Now we know clearly why, and for whom,
> we are working.
> Now, our aim is to serve the people.
>
> I came into the dock when I was a small child,
> So high.
> For sixteen hours a day, I crushed coke,
> Eating like a dog.
>
> The overseers, those bad persons, bullied
> the children,
> And misused the bodies of the girl-workers.
> The children lived in sheds together,
> On the waste-ground."

She touches here forearm, in a second's absence; eyes
staring for a moment in a pale face, and starting to attention.

> "When we see the new generation we
> are pleased,
> For we see our successors.
>
> We were called cruel names, 'coal-black
> ones',
> And beaten.
> A girl child, and a coal-crusher, as I,
> was nothing.
>
> I had no shoes to wear,
> Binding my feet with sacks.
> I thought of myself only as a coal-crusher,
> And had no rights,
> As a lowly person.
>
> Now, though we retire with our bodies,
> We will never retire in our minds,
> But will recall the bitter past,
> For our children."

She sits upright, careful hands placed together on her knees.

Flags flap red, and high-pitched, over the dockland streets,
and dockyards.

Here are fists and elbows; arms akimbo; clenched hands;
or, calm and spent, folded; and young men's and women's
delicate fingers and finger-tips, set firmly at the table-edge.

There is a silence, without stirring; and, in a sudden rising cadence, the room stands up, and all those in it.

94

Masts pass in the pearl-river, water fast-running, sky bursting and over-cast; darkening. In a small conservatory in the damped-dark river-gardens, men are talking and smoking.

There are girls together, approaching along the river-walk, in a clip and clack of sandals, slapping under the dark soles of their feet; the jostling elan of girls, in a crowding ardour of blinking and striding.

Masts and patchwork-sails stand under clouds, anchoring in deep milky water, for the evening. Old triremes, hulls and prows like ancient galleys, red-flagged, lie low in the river, unmoving.

Wrinkled varicosed ankles in old patched pumps; thin legs in short black galoshes; old men in a creeping shuffle, half-turning, stopping and staring; pass on slowly.

There are few people left now, on the promenade-benches. A mouth opens, and yawns. There is a lapping swell; an ebbing away, into night-damps. Anchored junks are rocking, lantern-lit.

These are tiny light-points, last reflections.

95

In the doorway of a shop, an old man, forehead touching
his knees, cradles in his crouched body a sleeping boy of four
or five. The colour-televisions play in bright array, while they
sleep or die, in their lights. At a late-night market restaurant
(a series of lean-to sheds, open to the street), slops mire the
eaters' feet. Amid them, an old man bends over a filthy bucket,
scouring dishes with a rag, almost asleep.

The multi-coloured neon blinks in a whirl of cars. 'International hostesses', 'nude-look waitresses', 'topless barmaids',
claim the hungering, dazzled eye. The 'New Life' offers balm;
but it is only a brothel's sign, above an open door.

The silence of a night street increases the sound of the
blood in the heart, of the heart breaking into anger, of action
and creation bursting through struggle, into being. Clawed
down by the beasts of capital into the gutter of Haiphong
Street, Hong Kong, an old woman, wasted, wraps her hair in
a white kerchief, preparing for bed. She has a mattesss to sleep
on, laid on three tea-chests, standing on the wet pavement.

A light rain weeps on us, ineradicable miniature vision of
this world's falling, watcher and watched exchanging glances.

THE BLACK LIBERATOR PRESS is a publishing off-shoot of THE BLACK LIBERATOR. Its purpose is to publish texts which, in the judgement of the Editorial Board, make a distinctive contribution to an understanding of contemporary World revolutionary changes; or which provide new evidence and analysis of the nature and impact of imperialism and racism, and of the international and domestic class struggles being waged against them.

TBL
PRESS